THE ONE THING AND SECRET OF LIFE

THE ONE THING
AND
SECRET OF LIFE

*A Step-by-Step Guide to Leading
a More Heavenly Life*

BOB CERAMI

YorkshirePublishing
www.yorkshirepublishing.com
Write Now.

ISBN: 978-1-947825-43-7
The One Thing and Secret of Life
Copyright © 2014 by Bob Cerami

Yorkshire Publishing
3207 South Norwood Avenue
Tulsa, Oklahoma 74135
www.YorkshirePublishing.com
918.394.2665

DEDICATION

I dedicate this book to anyone and everyone who wants to improve their lives and will no longer allow the words and expectations of others hold them back. To those who will no longer let religiosity or humanism clip their wings and keep them grounded. To those who want to be free to explore realms previously unknown. To those who want to seek and find answers to problems where they were previously lost and confused. This is for all those who want more for their lives than they were told they could have.

I dedicate this book to you, that one day you may find out for yourself what I was fortunate enough to find. I have spent many years working through the complicated maze and found a path that leads straight through the middle doing my best to simplify it and make it clear for you. There is a process so simple that a child, with all his innocence and purity of heart, has a better chance of understanding than a learned adult, who basically has to undo most of what he has filled his head with.

I dedicate this book to you, that you may discover your wings and soar into the heights of the most glorious places imaginable and freely walk through the gates and enter. I hope you will be able to transition from your intellect (your head) to your spirit (your heart) and discover all that waits for you. That someday you will see what has been waiting for you your whole life, something that only a few have witnessed.

I dedicate this book to you that someday you will become the person you were created to be and then help others find their way to see for themselves.

ACKNOWLEDGMENTS

I would like to thank all those who came across my path and helped a broken man stand back up, turn his face upwards and lead him to the Promised Land where he could discover a place to grow, overcome and be blessed. Many of the people I have met in my life were ground squawkers, who were fast to give their limited opinion, exert their control and complain about how life treated them. It was the few who found their way past this and were able to go beyond the walls and structures set up to keep us from seeing the expanse of the Truth that I thank. Those who cared more about their freedom and didn't let the opinions of others stop them from exploring while enduring harsh criticism, insults, mockery and rejection.

I thank those who care more about where they are going then where they are and have their eyes set on the goal having the conviction that nothing will stop them from arriving. You have found the place of blessing and have blessed others including me so I may find out for myself.

I acknowledge the explorer, the free spirit who will go to the ends of the earth and beyond to find the truth so they can show others the paths that lead to higher ground.

CONTENTS

INTRODUCTION

Did you ever wonder if there was one thing, some secret that could change your life for the better? Is it money, position, some object, belief, or thing that you think will bring you the happiness, peace, and joy you desire? For each of us, it can be vastly different, our aspirations so diversified. In essence, we can all be hoping and seeking something that will lead us to higher ground. However, is there one thing, some secret to life, that will hold true for all of us? A place where we can go and get our individual needs met and answers that we have been long seeking to the problems we face in our daily worlds? The answer is yes, and through this book I hope to reveal it to you so you can find out for yourself.

Why is it that so many people who practice some form of religion or have some philosophy seem so bound up, dysfunctional, and depressed? The answer may be that they are following the ways and words of man and haven't found the secret of life, the place where they can find out for themselves the answers they are looking for.

Every day we are exposed to enormous amounts of stress and negative influences from which we, succumb to illnesses, depression, and even thoughts of suicide. With all we see and hear through the media and what we may be experiencing in our lives, it is no wonder the sales of anti-anxiety and depression medications are going through the roof. You see, celebrities and the highly successful who seem to have everything, living the American dream, melting down on the path to self-destruction; they have the best the world has to offer, and yet it is not enough. There is something missing in their lives. The news of people going on rampages, killing others, terrorism, plus the rising anger we see in people around us is enough to put you in the fetal position. Where can you hide? It makes you want to look for a safe haven, but is there any out there? People are going nuts, and it doesn't seem to be getting any better. The worst part is it seems to be accelerating. Where do you go? Who do you turn to? What happens if everything we believe in fails? Then what?

Through this book, I hope to show you the path so you can discover the "one thing" that can turn your life around and restore hope and faith for not only you but those around you as well. Once you discover the secret for yourself, you can, and will, want to lead others to this place of rest. This is a place where they can find out for themselves what the "one thing" is and how to embrace it. So as each of us self-discovers what it is that will make our lives better and bring hope and stability to those around us.

Initially, it will seem like a lonely campfire in a deep and dark valley, but as more of us discover the "one thing," it will turn that once-dark-and-scary place into a valley that is illuminated by the fires burning within each of us now joined together. This once-dark-and-cold land, which seemed hopeless, will now be a valley of fire, a beacon of light for those to travel to and find safety and warmth. Yes, we can restore hope to ourselves, our family, those around us, America, and the world once we find the "one thing." Yes, I believe there is great hope for our future if we can recapture what made us great as Americans and as a nation.

The USA is my country, but America is my belief structure of morality, spirituality, and all my convictions that allow me to be free to explore what I choose. In my estimation, America is a spiritual nation, one nation under God! It is absolutely fascinating once you understand what is behind America. However, this is the subject for a different book which I may write at a later date.

In the movie *City Slickers*, there are three friends from the city who are in search of a greater purpose for their lives. They decide to go on a cattle drive and be a ranch hand for two weeks. Their lives in the city, whether married, divorced, or single seem to be stale to empty, and their pursuit of this adventure is to fill the void they are experiencing. They are looking for the answer to what may make them happy. During the cattle drive, the trail boss named Curly, who hates "city folk," has completely intimidated all the wannabe ranch hands. During one scene, Mitch helps Curly find some stray cattle and then deliver a calf. Because Mitch got down and dirty, Curly takes a liking to him. In the next scene, they are riding back some of the herd to the camp, and Curly lets Mitch into a secret. He says the secret to life is "this," and raises his hand with his forefinger pointed upward. When Mitch inquires what that means, Curly states, "The secret to life is one thing." Mitch looks perplexed, and when he asks Curly what the "one thing" is, Curly replies, "That's what you have to go figure out." Curly adds, "If you can, you will have purpose in your life." Then Curly dies! The rest of the movie is about these three friends trying to discover the "one thing."

This movie represents, for almost all of us, the frustration and dissatisfaction we usually feel about our lives and the pursuit for a solution to our emotional lack, our emptiness, and our search for something to fill it. We are all on a journey for that "one thing," that thing that will make us happy for the rest of our lives. We will search to the ends of the earth looking for the answer. Most of us will die by the search in total frustration and never come close to the understanding of what the "one thing" is. We will perish well short of the mark, which we could have reached only if we could have found the answer, what that "one thing" for us was, and the secret to access it.

Once you find the "one thing," you will come to realize how simple it is! You will wonder why it seemed so difficult to find, when all along there were signs pointing to it. People came along and told you about it, and you ignored it. Billboards advertised it, and you were too preoccupied with yourself to see past your tunnel vision to read the bold writing. There were volumes written explaining what it is and how to get there, and you never understood the words. Of course, you have the naysayers—those who will tell you it doesn't exist, or it is a waste of time because it is unreachable, or it is a fantasy, or blah blah blah. It is up to you to push past all the obstacles, the words, and follow the signs pointing to it, as well as follow those who have discovered the "one thing" that has changed them so you can come into your own understanding of it, and how to apply it to your life.

You see, the secret to the "one thing" is figuring out the maze. Once you do, it takes a few moments to get there. Actually, there is a path right down the middle of the maze, which once you know its secret will help you bypass a lot of confusion and difficulty in your life and bring you to a place of perfect peace and rest. When you are lost in the maze, it can make you feel hopeless and despondent and just want to lie down and give up. We cry out for help and there never seems to be an answer, yet the way is right in front of us; the answer is in our face. We just need to stop long enough to hear the answer and allow our eyes to refocus so we can see the way out of our own hell. Someone may come across our path who knows where the exit is; and if we are too proud to ask them for help and listen to their answer, we will be perpetual wanderers in a wilderness of confusion and frustration.

I tell you today, the answer to finding the "one thing" is no great mystery and has always been right before us.

It is so simple it is mind boggling, yet it is so complex, due to the programming of our own mind, which makes it hard to see and comprehend. Your mind is the veil that separates you from the "one thing," and the secret is to get it out of the way. If you stop trying so hard and slow down long enough, you just might bump into it. Once you do, and you learn to apply the principles, your life will never be the same. You will start to overcome all your problems and begin to enjoy life as it was meant to be. Once you know the secret, the "one thing" is all you need to have a life filled with love, joy, and peace. It will open up the gates of heaven and allow you to walk in the way you were meant to live. You will have purpose and fulfillment, and no matter what is going on around you, it will no longer affect you as it used to.

What if I told you that you can walk through the gates of heaven and explore heaven and return to the way you were created to live today, would you believe me? Most people think that you have to die before you hopefully can go to heaven, while others doubt its existence. But once you know the secret, you can find out for yourself and no longer listen to what others tell you. I will tell, as a fact, that the kingdom of heaven is available to you any day you choose. You can enter and explore all its wonders; you just need to know how to access it. This book is a step-by-step guide to help you find the gates and freely enter the most amazing place you can imagine, no matter what you believe right now.

PART I

THE QUEST

Your quest to find the "one thing" starts now if you so choose!

Establishing a Need

If you think you are fine, then you don't have
any need!

It is only when you come to the place where
you have the need to find answers that can help
you solve your problems.

Every single person on the face of the earth has
a desire and need for something grander, more
exciting and fulfilling than what we currently have,
whether we admit it or not. We all have a need for
improvement in our lives. Deep down there is a voice
within us crying out for change, we just need to recognize
it. For most of us, it is all too evident. We have the need
for help that can lead us to an improved lifestyle. For
others, they think they are fine just the way they are.
The first thing we all need to do is establish the need to
want to seek something that can lead us past our own
shortcomings and limitations and to a better place. We
have built our lives on false precepts, on external things,
and in the end they leave us lacking, wanting more.
Something deep down inside us cries out for the peace,

joy, happiness, and love that the material world doesn't provide. Things only give us temporary satisfaction.

We have built our own little lost worlds, our own kingdoms, which were supposed to give us all our desires while we live in this world; but eventually when it fails, we realize it doesn't work. So we start over again on another venture, seeking the satisfaction we didn't get on the last one; we think this must be the answer, and once again we come to the same conclusion. Over time, when we come to the realization that what we are building is no longer working leaving us frustrated, confused or even depressed and worse on medication. The problem is we don't know whom or where to turn to. In our hurt and frustration, we point our fingers and blame others for our circumstances. *It can't be our faults. We worked hard and gave it our best. We did everything we were taught.* The reality is we learned from a very low level system—one totally lacking in the things that will give us all the qualities of life we truly desire. This system has left us hurt, betrayed, and abandoned by the people we thought we could trust.

Eventually, everything we have tried comes to the point where we can no longer bear it, and we have realized we have the need for something—one thing—that can change our lives. We soon understand that the world of man has failed us, and everything we have been told, instructed, and read didn't work as it was supposed to. The model doesn't work because we built it without reading the instruction manual or listening to how others told us to build it. The pattern in which to model and build out lives has been clearly laid out since the beginning of time. An instruction manual giving us the steps to unfold any mystery which can help us build an improved and healthy life has been written long ago. We rejected this to trust in our own wisdom and the knowledge of others which have fed our intellect, the very nature that needs to die. Whatever we put our trust in is the result we get. Whatever we believe will be the extent of how our lives end up. Whatever we choose to see will be the length we can go.

Before we get going, I want to establish a point and set my intention straight. I have absolutely no problem with people who have attained material possessions like great wealth or position as long as they have discovered the "one thing" that keeps them balanced in all of what they possess in the here and now. If they lose these things, they will not lose their purpose and will continue to prosper in life no matter what they face. But for those who use their material possessions, position, or things to draw their identity from and use these things as their security and purpose, I hope this will speak to you. I write this book to hopefully show you that when these things fail you, you will ask yourself, "What do I have left?" It's a blessing to be wealthy or prosperous and have found some higher purpose as long as you have found the thing that gives you the security and peace to enjoy life, with or without these external things.

I include myself in the above statement, and I know ever day I have to deal with issues that prevent me from moving further along the path to the place where I can experience greater prosperity and happiness than I have now. There are some areas of my life that are good, some okay, while others need work, and then there's the ugly. If I only focus on what is right in my life, I will ignore or cover up what I don't like or want to see. I have to face the fact that I am full of it, something smelly, before I can move to a place of finding the peace and security I desire. I have to constantly ask what is in me that causes me to fall short of the mark and limits me from growing as a person—where are my weaknesses? why am I unhappy? what cripples me? why don't I have real friends? along with a host of others. I have to ask myself *why* in order to overcome my lack. It is only by questioning that you can begin to see; and once you see, you can overcome.

If I can come to a stronger position within myself and stand tall no matter what things come my way, it will affect those around me and, in particular, my family. I can help them just by my stability and strength and lead not only myself but others, making correct decisions in tough times. Once I discover the "one thing" and learn to walk in it daily and absorb it, then no matter where I go, it will spread to those around me and change the atmosphere—at home, at work, or wherever I go.

Let me ask you a few questions: How secure would you feel if America fell and there was complete chaos? What if the world was coming to an end, say in six months? How about if the financial system collapses and you lose all your material possessions? If your cozy little world collapsed, then what would you do? Join the growing line of people looking to get on antidepressants so you can numb yourself even more and ignore the pain and avoid the problems? Each of us has to come to grips that the utopia of a world we all aspire to see and hope to live in is fast falling apart. Are you well enough inside to deal with what may happen, or if any of the things above happen?

If not, is your solution to drink, take drugs, or find some other escape to bury you head in the sand and pretend it is not there? There is no running from fear. How far will you allow yourself to fall before you stop the madness and seek help? You have to stop, turn around and face it, and take it on until you conquer it, and only through the "one thing" can you get the strength to do it.

We have all had our heads in the sand pretending that all is well for too long and the problems are minor. Every day, the news is getting worse; and unless you live on some island by yourself, it is getting frightening. If events keep unfolding the way they are right now and continue to deteriorate the way they seem to be going, we are going to see people jumping out of windows and off bridges that will overshadow the great depression. Most don't know whom to turn to, and out of panic and fear, they will do something very stupid and rash and cause harm to themselves and perhaps others. We have to stop our pretense now and take a sober look at ourselves so we can come to a place where we need that "one thing" that can help us in the worst of times and even in the best of times. I am not prophesying anything here, only asking you *what if.* All I am asking you to do is look at yourself and see what you can do to overcome the deficiencies in your makeup that will cause your knees to crumble and fear from gripping you in perilous times. I am asking you to find a need that you have to find something more than what you have now and pursue the "one thing" that can lead you to a safe haven no matter what you face.

My goal here is not to give you a long list of end-time scenarios and Armageddon-type biblical prophecies and trip you into believing what I'm saying; you can see your fill of it on TV and the Internet. I don't think you have to look very far to see problems. Even in the best of times, we all face issues and see our lack. The problem during the good times is that we don't have any need to look at what's wrong with us or seek the guidance of others. No, we are too busy enjoying the ride. It's like a sleigh ride down a long mountain. It's great while it lasts. The only problem is that when you get to the bottom, you have to walk back up again. It is only when we hit bottom and look up at the high mountain that we realize the error of our way and the long journey ahead of us to get back up. Gravity has this way of pulling us down. It's only by hard effort and exertion that we go upward. Life is nothing more than an upward journey to get to the promised land if we so choose. However, as long as you think your life is fine, you are on the sled going the wrong way, a sled ride to hell for some.

I will make this point here and probably a few more times during this book. You have been given the right to choose life or death, heaven or hell, every moment of every day of your life. Right before you, the gates of heaven and hell are open waiting for you to enter, and by your choices you will. Once you know the *secret*, it will make it easier to choose to enter heaven and experience all its qualities and avoid the alternative. Lack of knowledge will prevent you from entering a higher place, but it is up to you to choose. You have to stop using the excuse "I didn't know any better." You've been told but you didn't want to believe. I write this book to reveal and show you the *secret* to enter the gates of heaven wherever and whenever you choose. Every action you choose has an impact where you will end up. If I find that some or many of my decisions are not healthy, then perhaps I should realize I have a need for something else.

When do I stop and realize I need help from someone or something else? When it is too late! If I have a drinking problem, do I wait until I get a DUI or hurt someone before I seek help? If I smoke, do I wait until I contract an illness before I seek help? If I am depressed, do I take drugs, cover over the pain, and avoid the help I need to feel good about myself and where my life is headed? No matter what problems you have, you need help now. Why wait for it to get worse? We all have to say, "I need help now and I need to find the 'one thing' that can help me overcome my issues."

Aside from myself and my own issues, perhaps there could be a need for me to help in the greater scheme of things that seem far beyond what I believe I have to offer. I might be able to make a contribution to my community, my country, or the world if only I could get out of my own way. I don't know how much you have to offer or how great your call is; but if you lay broken on the ground, you are useless. It is time to rise up and pursue the "one thing" that can give you the purpose you need to make a difference and bring change to yourself and a dying world that surrounds you.

WHERE DO I BEGIN MY SEARCH?

You must learn to look above the obvious layers
to find what lies underneath.
  Once you can see past the external, you will
begin to understand where to search.

The first place is recognizing that you have a need
for something else in your life that can take you
past all your frustrations and into a better place. Once
we come to recognize our brokenness through the many
hurts, rejections, and failures we experience, we are
more likely to start the search. If you have established
the need, the question now becomes "Where do I begin
my search?" Hopefully, through this book I can help you
identify that "one thing" and the path to it. Knowledge
is key to finding your way out of your confusion, and I
will give that to you today.

  As you scan the horizon looking for answers, you see
many possibilities and things that could be the answer
you have been looking for. The key is to not overlook
the obvious and the answer that has been in front of

your face all along. Just because you don't see it at this moment doesn't mean it is not there. You have to learn to adjust your sight to see past the material and look into what may be inanimate. In other words, you have to start looking past the external into the internal. Your search is more inside of you than on the outside. It is not in a place or time or thing. The *secret* lies within you.

I know you are probably thinking, *Well, that doesn't make sense. In the last chapter, you said there are many smelly things on the inside of me and that I need to get out of myself. I don't get it.* That is true, and you need to learn to deal with those things, but also on the inside are the answers which are currently covered over by the problems. In order to get out of yourself, you need to see past the problems and to the solutions. Yes, you have to get out of yourself, but stay within yourself. Your soul houses all of your emotions, both good and bad.

Within your soul is a mixture of emotions; a lot of confusion is going on within you, just like the weather— some days are good, some days are bad, and some days I don't know what to expect. Your mood swings are from "everything is great" to "my life is a mess." How can we experience both? Because in you, there is a mixture of both good and bad; and if we don't know how to control what will trigger our emotions, that is what we will experience. An external event or what someone says, either good or bad, is what determines what feelings stir up. The less control over your character, or what's going on inside you, the greater the mood swings you will experience.

So within me, I have a mix of good and bad, just like the cartoons where you see a character with an angel on one shoulder encouraging him to do what is right and the devil on the other shoulder demanding he does what is wrong. Yes, we have two voices going on, each contradictory, and the soft, still voice is the one we most likely need to listen to. Knowing how to discern which is the right voice or thought is something I will cover at length later. As well, I will also talk about your two minds, double-minded, through which you can perceive different types of thoughts through each mind. The key is to find that "one thing" that can help you sort all this out and give clarity to what you think and feel, and how to take control over it.

What we all seek is to think clearly in all situations and control what lies ahead of us no matter what. If we can learn to distinguish what is self-centered and what is not, then we can accept or reject thoughts that will determine our course of action. This is what I meant by "getting out of yourself"—stop being so centered on self and not looking outside of yourself for the answer. Taking control over thoughts is done through discernment of good and bad. You can only accomplish this through a model that can show you the difference. I am not talking about the obvious, but the subtle things in your soul that cause you confusion.

Aside from your soul, we also have your spirit, another part of you that has an internal perspective and is a great part of who you are. It is in the recognition of this side of yourself and the decision to seek to strengthen your spirit that will also play a significant part of discovering the "one thing." We were created with three parts, which are the *body* or material, the *soul* or mind and emotions, and our *spirit*. It's in the recognition and operation of all three that will determine the outcome or your life. Obviously, we recognize the physical and our soul through which we feel and think. What is not so obvious is the operation of our spirit within us. For most, it is asleep and needs to be awakened. You can ignore it all you want; it doesn't mean it doesn't exist. We also receive thought through either of our two minds—the mind of our soul or the mind of our spirit—which I will cover later. Again, discernment is needed, which comes from knowing how to listen to your spirit, your inner self.

We begin our journey in the recognition of what is inside of us, what makes us tick, and the operation of each part of us. Then we can start to take the jumbled mess churning on the inside of us and try to sort it out like some giant jigsaw puzzle with no picture to go by—a huge task, at best, and without the help of someone, or something perhaps impossible. It's like having your computer hard drive filled with bad programs, viruses, cookies, and all the crap that makes it dysfunctional or crash. You can't just format it and start all over because you will lose all the good programs. Imagine if your life's work was on that hard drive? The last thing you would want to do is erase everything. What you need is an expert, and perhaps the creator of the program, who can help you painstakingly go through each component of the program one by one so you both can remove all the bad stuff.

It's like a Jules Verne movie, only this one is called *Journey to the Center of the Heart.* That's the voyage you are about to go on, into the center of your heart, to see if you can find the "one thing" that can help you sort out the mess. It's not what you look like on the outside that matters but the condition of your heart. I know you have been avoiding it your whole life in fear of what you may find, but it is the first step in discovering your true self and the "one thing." You must take a long, hard, deep look at yourself to the core of your being and allow the process of discovering what makes you tick and why you are where you are. At first, you might be frightened at what you see and even deny that exists in you, but as you learn to see it, deal with it and overcome it, you will be very grateful you did. You will now be set free of a huge weight and burden from you life. The next one won't be so bad; you might even look forward to it.

The condition of the one influences the other. As you learn to set free the one, the other one is also set free. I am talking about your two natures. As you heal your soul, your spirit is set free. If you allow your soul to stay the way it is, your spirit can never experience the joys and wonders it was created to. Each broken pattern in your soul you learn to correct allows you to walk straighter and taller. It will be much easier climbing the high places as you learn to drop weight after weight. Where you will learn to go in your discovery of the "one thing" and where it leads will require you to let go of a few things and beliefs up front, and more and more as your journey continues. It is a lifelong process. I don't want to make it sound easy, because you will face and have to deal with some of the hardest things you could ever imagine. If you are unwilling, you will stay where you are and perhaps end up worse. If you like that forecast for your future, then stop reading and give this book to someone whom you think needs some change in their lives.

This trip is not for the weary. It is not for the lighthearted. You will see and experience some of the scariest and most glorious things along the way. There won't be a dull moment as long as you continue your journey and not turn back and return to your Egypt of captivity. There will be many temptations to get you discouraged and run away, but I tell you that the discovery of the "one thing" and your continued journey with it will lead you to some of the most amazing places you could ever imagine. You have no idea where you will travel or end up, but it will be much better than where you are today. I know the hardest part will be what seems like the endless wandering around the wilderness, but there are some very stubborn patterns in your life that don't want to go away and will do all they can to hang on. It seems like if you continue in this path to freedom any longer you are going to die. But you won't die, just the part of you that needs to. You must die so you may live the life you are designed to live. Don't ever be discouraged, but push on and resist all temptations to settle for less than you are called for, and should be. What lies ahead far outweighs all the pain of the journey.

Are you ready to start your journey into the unknown and take your first step? Commit yourself to at least finish this book because there may be some concepts and ideas that cut across the grain of your beliefs. Maybe they will go along the grain and reinforce your beliefs and push you along further than you have been able to go so far. Just remember that every vehicle created by man has its limitations; and when that takes you as far as you can go, you will need to find another to take you further along in your quest to discover what your life is all about. Just know that religion, what man creates, is the enemy of your spirit and will limit your walk and clip your wings so you can't fly.

CESSPOOLS

Learning to deal with what lies under the surface. Once you are able to face what stinks about your life, you will be on the path to overcome the issues that plague you.

Let's start with the ugly and stinky. Your life right now may seem like nothing more than a cesspool. Whether you want to admit it or not, deep down buried somewhere there is a pool that houses everything that is wrong with us. I will call it a *cesspool*. Let me show you how it operates in your life and its effects on those around you.

I remember when I was a young boy, my grandfather, father, and uncle had this huge hole dug in the ground with a backhoe, and they were laying cinder blocks on their sides so the holes were sideways. It was spring before the season opened to my family's summer resort in Upstate New York for a string of twelve rooms. As the curious kid I was, I asked them what they were doing. They told me they were building a cesspool so all the crap from all those rooms over there would come into here and leach into the ground. After it was done, they covered it with a big cement slab. So I asked why they did that, and they told me to keep the smell from the crap from all those rooms over there to be sealed. As long as the slab stayed intact and the earth around it wasn't disturbed, you could never smell anything from the crap from all those rooms over there. One day, I remember they had to dig a hole next to the lid of the cesspool to suck out all the solid stuff that had built up over the years that didn't leach out into the ground. What a horrible smell that came from that cesspool, and I ran as far away as I could get!

Here is how it operates in your life. Each of those rooms over there represents all the bad programming the world has placed in you from the day you were born until the present. All the crap from those rooms ends up in your heart. The liquids leach out into the earth, which is your soul. You cover it over with this big, thick cement slab, your facade, so no one can know it's there or smell what's hidden deep inside of you. As hard as you try to keep it covered, as the thick stuff builds up, you have to open a hole. The hole in the ground is your mouth. At some point, something is going to trigger what's latent inside of you; and no matter how well you think your cesspool is sealed, some nasty smell will percolate out of you mouth or through your actions. You will hurt or offend others. You will continue to sabotage your life. Out of the overflow of your heart, you will speak and act.

There is no hiding or containing it; it's just a matter of time before it backs up and it has nowhere to go but out of your mouth. You wonder why so many people flee because of the way you act or by what you say. Your family will love you no matter what; they got used to the smell and just ignore it and put up with you. Doesn't mean they like it. For some, even their families have to get away. It's really ugly stuff and no wonder so many of our relationships are strained or even ruined. My father used to tell my sister and me that his farts "smell like roses." Well, to him they might not have been so bad, but to us they stunk. We all want to believe that what is wrong with us no one else can see, and it isn't offensive. Even though we do our best to put our best foot forward and create this facade of wellness, even a child can see through it and recognize the smell beneath.

Hopefully, you don't think all I want to focus on is what is negative or wrong with you. My hope is to bring you to the realization that there is a side to each and every one of us that needs to be recognized and dealt with. Show me one person who doesn't have issues and everyone loves, and I will show you a perfect man or woman. I have never met one, and I am sure you haven't either. Our friends and the people we like to hang around with will have similar qualities, as we can share our likes and dislikes and find common interests.

All too often, we find people we can open our cesspools to, usually those who haven't run away and can take the smell because it is familiar to theirs. We can find great comfort in sharing our woes and problems and having a pity party to justify our positions. They can be drinking partners; talking on the phone or hanging out so we can talk about how screwed up the world is and everyone else and find someone to agree with us; "I wouldn't be in this position if it weren't for others or circumstances." It is real sad to watch these black holes of need suck everyone they can in to feel better about themselves. Hopefully, someday they will get desperate enough to look at themselves and come to the reality that it is no one or anything else but all their own making. Then if the need gets strong enough, they can open the lid to their cesspools and begin to deal with what's in them.

Sure others have hurt and wounded you, but it is up to you to overcome it, and you can.

The wisest man to ever walk the face of the earth, and I will tell you later why I make this statement, once said, "Pick up your cross and follow me." It means to let go of your problems, the things that hold you back, and leave your cesspool behind. The idea behind picking up your cross is to die to your old nature of self-reliance and self-destruction. It also means leaving behind all of the negative qualities of your old self which is laden with insecurity, anxiety, fear, depression, illness, and premature death, to name a few. It is like taking your old, heavy coat and hanging it on a nail on a post so you can cross to the other side to the "one thing" and realize all the promises that were given to you from the beginning of time. It's as simple as learning to walk away from your cesspool and following someone who can lead you to all your heart's desires. Keep in mind I said your *heart*, not your soul, and I will continue to show you the difference as we journey together toward the "one thing." He also said to "pick up your bed scroll and walk," which in essence means to deal with the problems that cripple you, roll them up, and put them under your arm and begin to walk freely where you couldn't before. Don't worry, you don't have to drag around that old mat for long; you will find a fire to throw it in and let them all burn.

If you choose not to find a way out of the cesspool of your own making, you'll end up on antidepressants, just like the rising tide of others so you can numb the pain and don't have to deal with all the things that capture your heart and cripple you. When you are in this place, it is like a death row sentence in which you are just waiting to die. Your quality of life is not good, and it will continue to darken thoughts in your mind that justify you rushing into death. I know; I lived it and experienced some of the darkest days of my life—depressed, on drugs, with thoughts of suicide, and in an institution. It can get real dark and scary, and there is a fine line between life and death, and the latter seems the better choice when it appears you have nowhere or no one to turn to. If things get dark enough, you will pull the trigger and slit your wrists. It's when you admit that you need help and find someone who can lead you out of this mess that will reverse your slide into the pit. Hopefully, you can look out and above this pool of despair and find the "one thing."

If you want to know how deep and wide your pool is, go to the mirror, look yourself in the face, and ask yourself: "How much time do you spend in your problems? How self-absorbed are you thinking the world revolves around you?" Try to get past the image you put on every day to cover your emptiness and look at your reflection in the pool to see who you really are. You have to lift the cover off the cesspool and look in. As you gaze at your reflection, you will see things come to the surface, and it is then you can begin to deal with them. As long as they are hidden, you don't know what they look like; but when your eyes adjust to see what you may have feared, you now realize it was not that big of a deal and the fix is simple. Our fear is of the unknown not the known. Once we see it, there is nothing to fear. We can now learn to deal with it and find a solution to overcome it.

Each of us has to come to terms with who we really are, or we will continue to sink deeper, as gravity pulls us down, like quicksand, in the cesspool of our own making. Every day of our lives, we have to resist gravity with great effort as it tries to pull us into our graves. I heard a saying, "Life is like trying to shimmy up a greased pole; once you stop trying to get to the top, you start sliding back down." There is no in-between or middle ground in this journey. Either you push forward and overcome all obstacles and enjoy a greater quality of life or die at the first obstacle in the road that stops you. So I say to you, roll up your bed scroll, pick it up, and let's continue our journey to the "one thing." Along the way, we will make an altar to burn your bed scroll.

THE SECRET

The journey begins. You must leave behind all that will weigh you down, for the journey is long. Once you understand that, there is a secret which will allow you to solve the puzzle of life and allow you to press on.

The journey begins!
Okay, enough said about what's wrong with you and all the problems you face every day in a messed up world. Now, let's go find the "one thing" that can make a difference in your life. Let me first begin by formulating the secret of the "one thing" and attempt to show you that what may seem to be obvious is not quite. It is hidden to the natural eye and mind, and there is a secret way of approach. I will attempt through the rest of this book to lay the foundation to the secret of life and path of approach to the "one thing." My goal will be to bring you into a full realization of the secret so you can pursue your purpose in this life and cross the finish line fulfilled. If I am not able to articulate my point well enough for you through my explanation,

then please forgive me for my shortcomings and for letting you down.

If you think this whole thing is about some methodology of religious or philosophical practice and belief, you are wrong. If you think this is about some intellectual understanding of God or some higher being, you are also wrong. I will liken it to say that if you knew the secret behind the Rubik's Cube, you can solve it quickly no matter what the combination is. Most of us have tried to figure it out without knowing the secret and have spent numerous hours getting, at most, a few sides to match while the rest is still jumbled up. After we get frustrated enough, we just lay it down on the coffee table and give up. This cube is nothing more than an exercise in futility. Only if you knew the secret to the Rubik's cube wouldn't it be simple to solve.

Life is nothing more than a Rubik's Cube, called the matrix of life, which without the "secret" is totally futile and frustrating. We can manage to get a few sides to match; and if we haven't gotten so frustrated and thrown it against the wall by now, we lay it down, incomplete, and give up. If you are satisfied with incomplete, then read no more. But if you want more, to go beyond where you have been able to go so far, then let's continue.

Then imagine some child comes over and picks up your discarded Rubik's Cube on the coffee table and starts twisting and turning it in a rapid fashion, and within a few minutes all the colors on all sides match. It is complete! In all your brilliance you couldn't come close, but this child did it in a flash. In total amazement and with your jaw hanging down, you ask him how he did that.

He says, "Once you know the secret, it's easy."

You ask, "Can you teach me the secret?"

He says, "Nah! It would take too long, and it is difficult for someone like you who is set in his ways and can only think in linear patterns."

You get defensive as you fight your ego, but your fascination to how this child could do what you couldn't outweighs ruining the moment and opportunity. "Please, can you show me the secret? I really want to know," you ask more adamantly.

He comes back at you with, "Only if you are able to change the way you think and get out of the way enough to see the secret." He continues, "You have to see the secret to solve the puzzle. You will have to change your perspective to see things in a different way, almost like that of a child."

You wonder, *Am I capable of change after all these years being locked into the same patterns to the way I think and feel?* Now you face a quandary. *Can I or can't I?* It's at this juncture in your search for the secret where you either pick up your bed scroll and walk, or lie down and wait for death.

The secret is the pathway to the "one thing," those pathways lost long ago. It is hidden from our natural eyes and can only be seen by our spiritual eyes. There is no one way or pattern to the "one thing." For each of us, the journey to the "one thing" is unique and personal. Each of our characters, from all the different programs, from all the different sources, is unique and could not be duplicated. You see, that's what makes the secret to the "one thing" so amazing; you can't create a religion or philosophy to make it work to accommodate all the diversity. Just like the cube with so many possible combinations and outcomes, the secret is far beyond any method anyone could come up with to solve the matrix of our lives except the "one thing." The "one thing" will give you the ability to see how to complete your matrix and the secret to the cube. The secret is not looking at it from your old way, but seeing it from another vantage point from outside of yourself. "You have to get out of the woods to see the forest," an old expression. The key is you have to see it! You change your view by going from your intellectual understanding to your spiritual mind and seeing by the eyes of your heart. If you can learn to make this transition, you will see it! This is the beginning of knowing the secret to life.

Bear with me as I take you on a side trail which will help me establish my point. I was raised in a loving family whose dietary knowledge was not the healthiest. I grew up with some of the best Italian cooking ever. Aside from my mom's and grandmother's great cooking, every summer we would travel to my family's Italian resort in the Catskills in New York. My uncle was the cook and the food was phenomenal. It was like a ten-week orgy of good eating. They knew how to cook good, *very* good. They just didn't know what was healthy for you back then. Proper nutrition wasn't even a concept in my circles. They learned these wonderful recipes that were handed down to them from generations of good cooks from Sicily. They would tell you, "These recipes are family secrets; don't tell anyone or they might steal them and make a lot of money off of us." Another issue with my family is they had a lot of unfounded fears. I used to think, *Why don't they go make a lot of money off of the family's secret recipes?* The reality is we all are delusional in thinking our secrets are so special. I grew up with a lot of ghosts in my closet and lots of baggage to carry around most of my life, stuff I am still working through today.

So my diet consisted of carbs for breakfast, carbs for lunch, and carbs for dinner with some bad fats mixed in. Guess what our snacks consisted of? Carbs! After a certain age in my late twenties, my diet started to catch up to me and I started to pack the pounds on and continued to do so until recently when I had to come to grips with my eating habits. What I perceived as good for me wasn't any good. I couldn't see the reality of how my diet was leading me to an early grave. My physique looks like a beer keg with arms and legs coming out the side with a head on top. I struggle with being tired, sluggish, feeling depressed, and lacking motivation most of the time. I was usually grumpy and irritable and found my comfort in my next meal. Needless to say, I wasn't having much fun or finding much joy in life.

I had to come to grips with this reality. It is an ongoing struggle as my patterns are strong and the roots of my dietary upbringing go deep. I am in the process of retraining my thought process and trying to see things differently. I started to go to an alternative medical doctor and nutritionist to help restore my body and get a handle on my eating patterns. They recommended all these natural food supplements and products and told me how to adjust my diet. I left, all motivated and excited, to make the change now that I saw things differently. But the execution was another matter. I had to give up most of the food I loved. After a short while, the rationalizations and excuses began: *It's just a bowl of pasta, it can't hurt that much. That bagel looks good, one won't matter. I need good Italian bread with my not-so-good cold cuts, but I added healthy veggies.*

Every day I made excuses to feed my flesh, the old nature full of deeply rooted and unhealthy patterns. I would go back to the medical center and the same pattern of attempted change followed, but the same rationalizations would persist. Instead of getting better, I was getting worse. I was making a lot of changes, but it wasn't enough. My weight was not going down and even inching still higher. I told my wife there was something wrong with the scale and we needed a new one. How hard change is and how funny we are as we continue to find ways not to, and our excuses are really creative. If it's not the scale, it must be my metabolism. Perhaps it is the atmosphere or my environment. Better yet, Earth's gravitational pull is getting stronger and making me weigh more.

Finally, they told me that if I wouldn't be more disciplined with my diet, I was wasting my money on the expensive products and office visits. I continued to go because deep down I really wanted to change and knew I had to push through. But as much as I learned and understood was as much as I struggled to implement it and take hold of it. I know what is right, but I continued to do what is wrong. In my most recent visit, the doctor told me I am on the verge of diabetes and had to cut out all bad carbs. Even though I had made great strides in cutting most carbs out, it wasn't enough. It was a wakeup call as my health and life depend on my choices. The patterns are strong, and it's an ongoing battle every day and every meal. If I continue in making the wrong choices, it will continue to cripple the quality of my life.

Now I eat a Zen fiber cake or protein shake for breakfast instead of eggs over easy with bacon and sausage and crispy home fries and good crusty buttered toast. Remove for breakfast, for lunch, it is salad and protein with a light dressing instead of a sandwich, thick, with cold cuts and lettuce, tomatoes and other veggies with mayo and mustard. Dinner had turned from pasta, rice, or potatoes with meat and a side of salad or veggies to salad, green vegetables, and lean meats. My all time favorite meal was a large pot of meat sauce, slowly cooked with meatballs, sausage, and other fatty meats over pasta or lasagna as the first course, followed by meat and potatoes and all kinds of other side dishes. I grew up with this as our Sunday feast where the whole family would gather together and eat. I used to stuff myself, go lie on the couch, and watch my favorite sports teams. I can no longer do this as I had to face the fact that this lifestyle was killing me.

They say you eat with your eyes. Well, I eat with my eyes, my nose, my mouth, my whole being as I totally gave myself over to food. I've got to learn to feed my body and not my face. I am making great strides into improving my diet and now realize it is a lifestyle change for the better. I realize I am not thickheaded but thick-natured. My old nature is dense and stubborn and doesn't want to change from years of wrong programming. Perhaps it is easier for others, but for me it is hard. Maybe one day I will write a cookbook to tempt you as well.

I've heard this saying somewhere along my journey, that if you walk back and forth on a wood floor long enough, it will create a groove. If you continue in this pattern, it will turn into a rut and be harder to get out of, and finally, given enough time, turn into a ditch that may seem impossible to get out of. Your situation may seem hopeless as you don't see a ladder or lifeline out. There is always hope and a way out if you feel stuck. You just have to see that way out and walk it step by step until change happens. Walking is discipline; acceptance is dying.

Learning the secret is one thing, but implementing it into your life is the challenge and the whole point of my story. I have to learn to cut the ties to the dead carcass that I drag around daily so I can travel on my journey and eventually reach my goal. We can all learn the secret that leads to life. Lazarus, rise! You are dead no more, now go walk.

The secret to life is to learn to serve the greater cause and not just your own. The more I serve my own cause, the worse the quality of my life, which in turn has a negative impact on my community. If I learn to serve the greater cause, then not only does my life improve exponentially, but everyone I touch can be impacted in a positive way. The next part of our journey will be to find your greater cause.

THE GREATER CAUSE

To continue the journey, you need to find a
cause greater than yourself.

Once you are able to see the larger picture, you
will come to realize how minor your problems
are in the greater scheme of things.

In order for you to get out of yourself, you need to find
a cause in your lifetime that is greater than you. The
first step in finding the greater cause will be to recognize
your spiritual nature, which is you higher nature. It
will be from this vantage point that you will see things
differently. Your perspective of life will change and your
ability to live life will vastly improve. You will learn to
see that there is more, so much more, than the little
niche you have or are trying to carve out for yourself
while living on earth. Our best is still limited and finite.
If you so choose to get beyond yourself, you can tap into
the infinite. The views and vistas you will see along the
way will be beyond anything you could imagine and,
once you find the "one thing," will be limitless.

It's up to you to explore! Don't ever listen to those
who choose not to see and limit their experience to the

natural world or the here and now. Those whose whole philosophy is based on the lower plains of life are blind, and their goal is to limit as many people as possible to justify their lowly view of life. They wrap themselves in the pride of how intelligent they are and how polished their arguments are so they can squash your spirit and keep you grounded. In reality, their spirit has become so atrophied all their reality is in their intellect. If you could see these people in the spirit, you would see a being like an alien whose cranium is oversized and too large for its body. This is the very nature that needs to be put to death so your spirit can be free.

One of my favorite all-time books is *Jonathan Livingston Seagull.* There was something that drove him to look beyond his lower nature, which was just living to fulfill the basic needs of life. He was compelled to find something more, some purpose higher than a meager existence, to fight for scraps of fish and to follow what he was told to believe by the council flock. There had to be more to life than the status quo, and Jonathan was on a mission to find the secret to his higher nature and the greater cause. The council flock warned him that his behavior was unproductive and against the denominational rules of the flock, and he needed to stop it and accept his role in the flock. Jonathan cared more about his purpose than the rules of the flock, which would have clipped his wings and left him grounded and maybe on antidepressants. He continued his pursuit to find his higher nature and was deflocked, excommunicated, and banished to the lonely places.

All alone, he continued his search for the greater cause and to perfect his higher nature. After he accomplished his greater purpose, he became radiant; and when he landed on the beach, other gulls were drawn to him. Eventually, the council flock took him back in, and he showed them the greater cause for their lives. By pursuing the greater cause for his life and finding the "one thing" that could make a difference, he was able to share the secret of life with others and impact the world around him.

What do you think about your life? Do you believe there is a greater cause for your life, something that can lead you higher than where you are right now? Have you asked yourself what it may be? Is there something burning deep down that cries out for more than you have accomplished? To answer these, you need to stop rationalizing and get out of your own way. You have to look beyond your own need to exist and break the chains that have been placed on you by others. Like Jonathan, you have to answer the call to want to know your higher nature. Your need to know has to outweigh your need to exist. If not, then the council flock, those around you, will dictate the outcome of your life, and you will fall way short of the greater cause and your true purpose.

What could that greater cause be? Where do you begin to look? I am sure you, like me, have tried many different ways and things presented to us and most, if not all, have left us lacking. Philosophies, religion, community, and government service, any method of the most brilliant minds have let us down and usually caused us to go away hurt, confused, and rejected. Many have even gone to the ends of the earth, climbing the highest mountains, to find that their old way of life is waiting for them when they return.

Pursuit of accumulating great wealth with the notion of helping others can also be nothing more than chasing rainbows and an excuse to fulfill our own lust for things. We listen to all these wonderful men and women who seem to have the answer; and after we decide to follow them for a while, we hit the wall of limitation as their method can take us no further. When you follow men, with their limitations, eventually you come to a dead end. Many of the things we pursue are good and have great causes behind them, but as brilliant as man can be, we soon find out their limitations. When they take us as far as they can and the program ends, our yearning for more starts again. It's like a good movie that captured you for a while but ended and left you hanging and wanting more. So they go ahead and create a sequel which is usually never as good as the original. Our quest begins again once we get over our hurts and frustrations, and learn to forgive and let go of all those who failed us.

There is nothing worse than someone who sells you a greater cause and you find out in the end that it was their cause. Be careful not to let the hypocrite stand in the way of you and the greater cause for your life, because there is no shortage of them out there. Most people end their search here as they are unable to forgive those who have led them astray and hurt, leaving them disillusioned. I know; I have been there, and it takes a long time to get over these feelings and arrive at a place where you can trust again. I will make you a promise—that if you are able to follow what I am trying to show you and find the "one thing" for yourself, you will never be let down or disappointed. I am not asking you to follow me but to allow me to show you the place you can discover it for yourself and make up your own mind. Just bear with me to the end of this book and see if the journey was worth your time.

Here is the first clue to the "one thing." It is learning to return to the way you were originally designed to walk and live. You have to learn to walk the walk and not talk the walk. You can believe in something very passionately and want to be there, but at this point, all you know how to do is talk about it because no one showed you the path and you don't have the ability at this time to experience it. So you talk about where you would like to walk. Just like the way I approached my diet, I talked the walk instead of walking the walk to my goal. As I start walking, things are changing for the better. Most people talk about their beliefs but haven't found a way to come face to face and experience firsthand the object of their belief. They read about it, hear about it, and even may experience from a distance. But I tell you, there is nothing like standing in front of it and seeing it firsthand and learning to walk with it.

You will arrive at your greater cause when you learn to walk upright and stand tall in your spiritual nature and not hunched over and broke down in your fallen nature. The longer I walk upright, the stronger I get. My ability to climb into the high places increases. As I continue to work out a correct diet for my body, it will heal, and eventually I can return to eating some of the foods I overindulged in in the past. It is time to explore the two natures, because once you understand it from this perspective, you will be able to learn to walk more freely to the "one thing." Once you learn to separate your thoughts and recognize the source from where these thoughts come from, it will make your journey that much easier. The way you walk will be determined by the way you think. Thoughts are powerful and they control you! Your mind is the veil that prevents the light from shining on the pathway that leads to high ground. Once you learn to rend the veil, everything opens up to you.

I discovered something over thirty years ago which became my greater cause. No one was talking or teaching about it, and when I approached them, they looked at me like I was nuts and way out there somewhere, not in touch with reality. As I listened to these knowledgeable people, the council flock, it became apparent they were keeping me from pursuing what I saw and experienced firsthand. The more I denied it, the stronger it became, and I had to go after it. During those many years of solitude, like Jonathan Livingston Seagull, developing the ability of flight, I was able to understand the concept or the "one thing." It took me over those thirty years to be able to make enough sense out of it, to be able to clearly present to others and show them the way to it. Yes, I had to overcome the limitations of man-made institutions and go beyond where very few were willing to go, and it is my cause to take you past the limitations placed on you by others. My greater cause is to show you the way to the truth for your life.

To find your greater cause, you have to learn to cast off the restraints and limitation placed on you by man. What you have been told by others is nothing more than a life sentence of mediocrity and compromise. In you, there is that nature that cries out for more. You sense the yearning for greater things, and every day you live with the frustration of where your life is today and not knowing how to satisfy its call. The big question is: How do you satisfy the desire to something greater when everything you tried left you short of the goal? Whether you believe in God, follow a religion, or have been taught some philosophy on how to find the higher call, most likely you have run into the human side of man and found it controlling and hypocritical. This is the veil of separation you must find your way past in order to continue your pursuit of the greater cause. Very few people are willing to go past the veil due to the cost, which is a complete laying down of your old nature.

I just want you to know that I hate religion as much as most of you do, and it is something I have battled most of my life. The realm of man has grossly misrepresented the realm of God. Not only misrepresented, but in many cases, used God for his own cause and gain. It is my intent to show you how to get past this. I will show you the secret pathway that leads past the many institutions of men, the very ones that claim they are the way. You will learn to shatter their limitations over your life so you can walk freely and without limitation in the realm of God. Throughout the rest of this book,

I will prepare you to be able to walk in *the way* that leads to the heights in God so you can discover your greater cause. I will show you how to leap and bound into the high places. You will see views and vistas you never imagined possible that will leave you breathless.

Before you can walk freely into the places I have told you about, I need to lay some foundation stones for you, and I will start with your two natures. I will now take you through ground school and prepare you to fly into the realm where eagles fly. The gates of heaven are opened to you, and you have the right to enter now. You don't have to wait to die, you just need to know how to.

THE TWO NATURES

If the model is broken and you can't find another one that works, you need to refer to the manual to fix it. Once you are able to see how the original was designed, it will be easier to fix what doesn't work. It is realizing that we live with two natures and knowing how to allow the one to overtake the other so we can live life as we are supposed to.

I have heard it said that if you have a model that you want to restore, find one that is working and copy that one. If you can't find a working model, then you need to go back and find the instruction manual and see its original design. Unfortunately, in this day and age, who can you turn to that is a working model of life according to the original design? I don't know anyone, do you? Even those whom I would consider highly spiritual or enlightened have serious issues. As wise as they can appear in one way and have the ability to help you, they are as broken and dysfunctional as they can be in another way being of no use to you. I believe we are all in the same boat—broken and looking for answers.

We search high and low looking for the answers that can help us improve our lives in the here and now, and all we find is others like ourselves.

Hopefully, through this chapter, you will come to see there is more to you than meets the eye. The recognition of the two natures will be a key for you to understand so you can go further in your journey to find the "one thing." In order to distinguish the differences of your two natures, you have to learn and understand the original design of that which you were created to live by and live in; as well as what went wrong, why it is broken, and how to fix it. You will need to understand what is operating in you and causing you to remain disjointed and feeling out of control in areas of your life. The key to fixing those problems will be for you to be able to see it, and once you do the solutions will come. You need to learn to enter that realm where you can receive understanding and revelation about your issues and how you can solve them. Everyone is different, so what I may find may be different than what you may need. Yet underneath it all, there is a common thread that works for all of us.

Let me introduce to you the author and designer of your higher nature, that which you were created to live in and by—God! Yes, God is also known as the Creator of life. If you're into evolution, which has a low view on life slithering out of the sea on its belly and can't get past the limitations of that whole concept, you might as well burn this book or give it away, because it will do you no good. But just because you can't see it now doesn't mean you can't. Your spiritual eyes are atrophied, like a muscle you haven't used, and needs to be worked into shape for the journey. Our goal is to seek the highest views of life you can attain. If you can take an objective look at what I am about to show you no matter what level of faith you may have, you will find that once you understand the original design for you, your growth will never end.

As I mentioned earlier, the Rubik's Cube has a secret to solve it quickly. In order to solve the Rubik's Cube, you must learn and study the secret and understand how it works and then, more importantly, apply it. In order to solve your own cube, you have to learn the secret, study it, and then learn to painstakingly apply it and walk it out until you reach the goal. Whether you believe in the cross or not will not get you closer to the secret of solving your cube. It's in the application of the cross and picking it up and following. The cross is nothing more than making the transition from one nature to the other. At the cross you lay down your carnal nature, and as you pick it up, you are walking in your spiritual nature led by the Spirit of God. It is about learning to transition from one nature to the other. Every day when you wake up, you start in your lower nature and must battle to get into your higher nature doing all you can to remain there. The forces of gravity are constantly trying to pull you down back into your lower life form.

The greatest "Rubik's Cube" we will ever face, for those who choose to try to solve it, is the Bible. Once you know the secret of the Bible, with all its great mysteries, you will be on your way to solve your life. Remember what I told you, that only you can solve the mystery of your life. As Curly said, "The secret to life is the 'one thing,' and only you can figure it out." Others can only help you along the way to keep on going and lift you up when you get discouraged. How do you unlock the mysteries of the Bible? I am about to show you. Don't try to Google it, you won't find it there. As in the cube, the Bible has many layers which you need to work through to get to your starting point on how to solve it. Once you learn to master that level, then you go to the next and apply each layer in its necessary order.

The Bible is nothing more than an instruction book to life, and you will see how simple the secret is and also why the greatest intellects and scholars who study it their whole lives can't figure it out. It is so simple that only the simple can see it. "…because you have hidden these things from the wise and learned, and revealed them to little children" (Matthew 11:25 NIV). Your intellect or fallen nature is the wise and prudent, and your heart or spirit has the simplicity of a child. When you try to figure it out from your intellect, which is your fallen nature, it is like trying to solve the cube without the secret. The Bible was written by people who operated in the realm of eagles, the Spirit, and to people who can hear with their spirit. The secret code of the Bible is nothing more than understanding the heavenly language it was written in. The words are in my natural language, but its meaning is understood clearly by my spirit through the Spirit. It doesn't matter what translation you use because your spirit can transcend words as God will reveal to your heart what the true meaning is of each scripture.

I am trying to draw a parallel here. You can either operate in your natural man or your spiritual man. Unless you know how to live in and by the Spirit, you will default to your natural nature. Understanding of the Bible, God, and the meaning of your life can only happen in your created nature. The natural man can only understand natural things, while the spiritual man understands spiritual things and the language of the Spirit.

Let's go back, way back, to the first model, Adam, in Genesis. It is here we see the creation of the two natures and how they operate. This is a key to your understanding so you can begin to solve the puzzle. This is the beginning of the secret to the "one thing." I will try to make this as simple as possible for you, without getting into theology and a lot of overlay. A part of you seeing it will have to come to you through revelation by God into your spirit. You will have to open the eyes of your heart. This will open the windows of heaven for the light to come in and clear up any confusion about who you are and who you are created to be.

In the beginning, God created man in his image, in his likeness to rule over the earth. This is our spiritual DNA. We were designed to live in perfection where there was only good and to have relationship with God and walk with him and talk to him in the garden in the cool breeze of the day—a place where there is nothing wrong, no problems or issues, and nothing to worry about. It was all good back then. We walked with God with our created nature or higher nature—our spirits.

In the middle of the garden were two trees—the tree of life and the tree of knowledge of good and evil. One led to life, and the other led to death. Even to this moment, today you still get to choose which tree you will eat from and what nature you will feed. So choice was given by God. You can choose life or you can choose death. Quite simple, isn't it? Perhaps not at this time, but I hope you can see the simplicity of it. So Adam and Eve are walking around the garden and everything is cool, and they are happy and loving life. They got all the money they need, their bank accounts are full, there is plenty to eat, and the cost of living is low. All they had to do to keep this lifestyle was to make correct choices—eat from any tree, including the tree of life, and your life will remain easy and light; but don't eat of the tree of knowledge, or things will get real hard and complicated, and the stresses will lead to death.

So they got snaked into and decided to eat of the tree of knowledge to see what would happen. Were they in for a rude awakening! Their self nature was born, an independent spirit which relied on its own intellect and knowledge and reliance on self. Self-centeredness and self-absorption were born, the two evils we will battle to overcome. This began the separation from God, and the perfect union of a healthy and pure lifestyle was broken. The self nature can also be called the fallen nature, carnal nature, lower nature, but it turned into the beast nature, where we had to put the skin of an animal or beast on to cover our nakedness, which before was no problem.

Then God asked them who told them to eat of this tree, and the blame game started. She said, he said. What was once good now became bad as the identity of self and the intellect of knowing started to grow. It grew to the point where it dominated our thoughts and overshadowed our spiritual mind. Thus, self-centeredness was born and the fallen nature was created, and it is fed from every thought from the tree of knowledge. God created the higher nature, and we created the fallen nature through choice. Everything we are experiencing today is our doing via the tree we choose to eat from.

They were booted out of the garden, and the entrance was blocked by an angel with a flaming sword. From that time on, they were relegated to work by the sweat of their brow and through pain and suffering struggle for their survival until they died. They were no longer allowed to eat of the tree of life in their fallen nature and were separated from God as long as they remained in this nature. However, God also designed into his plan a way for man to overcome this nature and be redeemed—which will be my goal—to show you the path to restoration. As long as we remain in the carnal nature, our relationship with God is from the outside of the gates and at a distance. No longer could we walk with God, in that perfect place of love, talk with him and experience the greatness of his creation, unless restored.

Man's spirit didn't die; it was just pushed aside as the beast nature became stronger and took over control of the higher nature and determined the course of one's life. The longer mankind walked away from the garden, the more distant God became to the point of many not even believing in his existence. Self-rule dominated our thoughts, and we created structures to control others to keep their beast natures in check. Some sort of law and order had to be created, laws to rule the beast and keep him in check. Mankind separated even further into many different kinds of cultures, languages, nations, and religions and created structures to accommodate their beliefs. Further and further we drifted from the place of creation and into separation from God and one another, until we arrived to where we are today. For some, it is pretty hopeless and frightening. The good news is there is a way back into the garden where you can eat of the tree of life once again and begin the process of healing and restoration. I will show you how to walk with God, face to face, and talk with him about your life.

Your two natures are your created nature or your fallen nature; your higher nature or your lower nature; your spiritual nature, or your carnal nature or flesh. One is spiritual which leads to life, and one is carnal which leads to beastly pursuits and death! Your spirit is fed from the tree of life, while your flesh is fed from the tree of knowledge. If you choose to seek and know the differences between the two, you will begin to discern how each operates and the controlling forces behind them. It is from here that you must learn to get out of yourself—out of your own head, your fallen nature— and start your journey back to and through the gates to enter the place your life was designed for.

As there are two natures, there are also two thought processes. Each nature has a mind of its own, that's why we can be double-minded. The angel on one shoulder and the devil on another is what we juggle every day in processing our thoughts. Each mind is a window into your soul through which you will feed either nature. Your carnal mind is your intellect where you hear through your head, and it is dense and stubborn and resists change, like a spoiled child. Your spiritual mind is the still quiet voice that lies within and it's heard from inside your heart. You attain knowledge through your intellect and wisdom through your heart. That is why some of the greatest theologians who try to understand God and the Bible through their intellectual minds miss it completely and fail to know who God is. That is why they sound like a hollow barrel. You can only know God through your heart. That is the place of redeemed relationship with him. In a sense, you must "cut off your head" and kill the carnal mind so your created mind can once again think for you and lead you back to life and hear from God.

I had a vision in the early nineties in which I saw kind of a steer skull with a very large cranium, while the rest of the facial structure was small, lying in the desert. I was riding my horse when I came upon it and I asked God, "What is the significance of this?"

He said, "It was the skull of the beast and carnal mind," and that, "You need to shatter it."

I thought, *Why is the cranium so oversized?* Before I finished the thought, the answer came back that it represented how the intellect had grown to an abnormal size and overshadowed the rest of the being. I took my sword out and began to strike it over and over again without even forming a crack in the skull. I then moved my horse in position, and he reared up and began striking at it with his powerful hooves. Finally, it cracked open and the skull fell away. Inside was a pool of liquid.

I thought, *Man, this was hard to break through.* Immediately a thought came back. *This represents the carnal mind which is dense, stubborn, and resistant to hearing my voice. It takes repeated blows with truth to crack the skull open.*

As I looked into the pool, I asked, "What is this?"

He said, "It is thought." He went on to say, "Thoughts control your every action, and you must learn to discern what thoughts are from me and what thoughts are not."

As I visited the place of the skull and carnal mind in my meditative time with God, he continued to reveal how it operates in my life. The roots go very deep and the programming is strong, and it is an ongoing process to see all the tentacles of this nature, how they control me, and how I must battle to overcome them. It was during these times I came to understand that our thoughts control our actions. Our thoughts come from the tree we choose to eat from. You can choose wisdom, life, or you can choose knowledge, death. During the rest of this book, if I seem to repeat points or get redundant, it is because your carnal mind needs *repeated blows* before it will open up and see the truth.

Moses was a perfect example of someone who had it all in the natural, being a worldly prince for the first forty years of his life. In spite of it all, there was a deep yearning for more. He spent the next forty years of his life overcoming the first forty years of programming from the worldly system he grew up in. As he worked to overcome his old nature, he was able to ascend up Mount Zion and visit with God and have his burning bush experience. As he stood before the flames, it continued the process of burning off his old nature which allowed his created nature to reemerge and strengthen. During that time, he was made ready to follow the hand of God and then go back into Egypt to lead God's people out of captivity and toward the promised land. The next forty years he led this stubborn and resistant people around the wilderness. The longer they complained and resisted from laying down their old nature, the longer they had to wander. It took forty years for them to die off one way or another so the next generation could enter back into the promised land.

You see, the faster you can learn to deal with your carnal nature and put it aside is as fast as you can return to your promised land and enter back into its gates. You can kill that old nature completely, but it will be a lifelong process by spending much time before the burning bush and fire of God. In the meantime, God allows us to lay it down or repent and walk in the Spirit with him. As you learn to walk with him spirit to spirit, you will take on his nature. It is a journey from imperfection to perfection. I will show you how to do this as we go along in "The Seven Steps." First we must understand the three realms in which we can walk and the operation of each.

As we have two natures, we also have two creations. We have God's creation in which we are still able to walk in and enjoy all the qualities of that kingdom. A place where everything is perfect and there is only good. The place we can visit and eat of the tree of life and start the restoration and healing process over our minds, emotions, body, and environment. "The kingdom of God is at hand" means it is right in front of your face, and you can enter and experience it just by turning the internal switch going from your carnal mind to your spiritual mind. Once you understand how to flip the switch, you can enter in a flash. It's that simple! That is the secret in a nutshell! Learning to flip the switch is also one of the most important points in discovering the "one thing." Did you ever wonder why some days are heavenly and other days feel like hell? I sought the answer to this question for a long time and finally realized it was through whatever nature was in control of me, thus would be the fruits of that nature I would experience at that moment.

Now on the other hand, you get to live in your own creation. The other creation is what mankind has manufactured to in all of his wonderful brilliance of their collective carnal minds. Look around to see how much security, peace, prosperity, joy, love, hope you can find. Where is the utopia, the fountain of youth, the place you can safely retreat to? America is the last bastion of some sort of hope, and its candle is fading fast as it has turned its back on God. If America falls, what's left that isn't lawless? Aside from a worldly kingdom, look at the state of our environment and how we have abused the resources in our greedy lust for more to feed the self. Our atmosphere and air quality is deteriorating, our water supply is becoming toxic, our food supply is filled with chemicals, and our medical system is designed to keep you sick. Your nest egg is merely a thin shell which anyone can dip their beaks through and suck your egg dry, leaving the shell. This is a mere synopsis at how our self-fulfilling creation is designed to feed off the flesh of others and drink their blood. To say the least, it is looking bleak for our future generations, unless we do something now.

What do we do? Whom do we turn to? Obviously it's not man, as you can look no further than to see what his creation looks like. If you can't see it, mankind in his fallen state is nothing more than a cancer to the earth. Don't believe me, just look around and do the math. If the earth were a body, after examination, the doctor would say it's terminal and it doesn't have much more time to live.

We don't have much more time left before we become critical mass and destroy ourselves. The old order must be replaced by the original order to the way things were designed to operate here on earth and for mankind. Tensions are getting so high right now that in a flash we can push the button and end civilization on earth. Don't you get it, man? We are at the end, and the hourglass of our world has a few grains of sand left in it. However, we can turn it around if we choose to turn from our way and get his way back into our lives, governments, and world. The hope of the world lies in you, in your higher nature. Your role to save the world is to change yourself and return to the state God created for you. The more of us that get it, the brighter the flame of hope, and the brighter the light to change what we have created so we can turn it around.

It is time to pick up your bed scroll of your broken and crippled nature and walk in your higher nature with God in his original design for your life. Your choice lay there—die or get up and walk and live. Choose life, your spiritual nature, and live; or choose self, carnality, and you will surely die. God gave us the authority to rule and reign over the garden, which through our choices we will govern and create the environment we will live in. He started us off with a perfect model; and as messed up as it may be now, there is hope to restore it. It's at this point you will need to decide which nature you will follow. Will you take the low road and continue to fulfill the desires of your flesh, or will you take the high road and learn to put the beast nature to death and fulfill the desires of your heart?

PART II

THE GOAL

Traveling to your destination where the "one thing" resides and getting to know how it applies to your life.

THE THREE REALMS

It's important to understand the different atmospheres we are able to walk in and how to navigate through each one, considering the terrain you will travel though in order to reach your destination and avoiding potential pitfalls.

In order to reach your destination, you need to understand the terrain you will encounter and how to navigate through everything that will come across your path. You must know how to plot your course, or you may end up in the bottom of a ravine. You can't pull into your local gas station to buy a map for this trip or MapQuest it. If you were going to make an attempt to climb Mount Everest, it would be wise to hire a local native who knows the mountain intimately, who has ascended and descended it many times, help you plan your route and how to pack for all the elements you may encounter. This chapter is designed to lay all the necessary foundation blocks for your journey upwards, to the very heights in God. We are leaving the low places, and from now on, we will be spending our time focusing on the views from the third realm. This whole book is a journey upwards to the place of our destination, the third heaven and the "one thing."

It's all uphill from here. You will need to shed all the unnecessary weight you can to continue your ascent to the top of the mountain. Don't try to take your baggage, it will hinder or perhaps stop you. Please check it in at the bottom of the hill. I will show you how to park your old nature on the side through the seven steps, while your renewed nature takes a trip—a vacation—from all your everyday problems, to enjoy all the vistas and places of rest and refreshment. All your fears, worries, anxieties, and phobias will melt away in the solitude and security of the heights, and you will find real peace. You know the peace that everyone pretends exists and wants here on earth, but in spite of all their efforts, protests, and holding signs up, it just keeps getting worse. "Give peace a chance," they sing the song in protest to the many wars. What a bunch of crap! Without God, there is no peace. In this place, you will find the real deal— genuine rest and peace. You will return feeling so much better, and your heart will yearn to go back.

The three realms relate to our three parts. The first realm relates to our body or natural man through which we maintain our physical health. The second realm relates to our soul, mind and emotions, which has great influence over what we feel and think. The third realm relates to the spiritual side of ourselves and the place where we learn to nurture that part of us. As we are three parts, our world has three levels that coincide with how each part is designed for us to live. Not understanding how to walk through each level will severely hinder our growth as a whole person. You were not created to be a one-dimensional creature but a three-dimensional person—a complete being that can walk freely through all three realms.

As there are three realms, there are also three voices. It will be critical for you to understand how they operate as you walk through each level. These internal voices can either assist you in your journey or discourage you and turn you back to the lower places. These voices influence your thoughts and emotions, depending upon which tree you eat from. You will learn to know if it is that of a guide who will assist you through the trials on your journey, or the voice of the council flock who wants you to turn back so you accept your hopeless situation. It is as important to understand who you are listening to as much as knowing the terrain you will face. Lacking in either of these two areas will stop you in your tracks, and a combination of the two will set you on a crash course for death.

The first realm is the natural world we live in. It is the earth, the sky, the stars, the air we breathe, the water we drink, the people we come in contact with and everything else we touch, see, hear, smell, and taste with our natural senses. It is also known as the first heaven or first dimension. It is the material reality we live in every day. This world is hard and dense and the most obvious. This is where realists and scientists draw their conclusions that this is all there is to life. You live your life here and now, so make the most of it, and then you die. How sad and unfulfilling. No wonder why there is so much hopelessness and why so many are on meds.

You get to choose whatever reality you want to live in. You can stay in the lower, more dense levels of life, and that is all you will ever experience. It's part of God's design that you get to choose whatever reality you want to live in and experience. Your choices here will form your belief structures and determine the course of your life. You can believe only in the here and now, and your reality will be limited to what you can see or touch in this world. Your reality can also go from believing in God from a distance or seeing him face to face. If you believe God is infinite, who offers you infinite possibilities, then as you walk with him your reality will constantly unfold and expand.

The first heaven is the place where we dwell with our natural beings and is where we need to learn to find a balance between all three realms. This is the realm where God came to us to save us from our own plight of suffering and death through his son's. It is the realm of God incarnate through Jesus to come into a fallen world by breaking the ties that held us down, showing us the way through the second realm and into the third realm. This is also the place where we learn about the things of God with our natural minds by listening to others who teach us about God, reading his word, learning to make sacrifices, and water baptism. It is where we learn to overcome our deficiencies through the cross and by washing them away through symbolic water baptism. This is where our outer man experiences the things of God in the natural.

The voices we hear in this realm are those of other people, their opinions, as well as our own. It is our own internal thought process where we listen, learn, and develop our belief structures for how we form our model of life. The voices from this realm have great influence over us; they can cause us to either be free or in bondage for much of our lives. Most of these voices work against us as they are self-serving, pretending to seek our well-being but are for their own gain. Much of our fears, phobias, and physical and mental illnesses come from the voices that speak into our lives from this level. It is crucial for each of us to find the place where we can truly know who we are so we can fend off those voices that seek to stop us from knowing the truth and, ultimately, to destroy us. As you find the "one thing," you will find the place where your identity can be developed; where you can shed off all the things you were told that are false from the voices in the first and second heavens.

The second realm or heaven is the unseen fallen spiritual realm. This is the atmosphere where both demonic and angelic spirits operate and vie for our attention. Yes, it is where cartoons get the notion of an angel on one shoulder, while a devil is on the other speaking into your ears. Don't take this lightly; this is exactly what is going on moment by moment in your life. The voices from this realm are strong; especially those that have inroads into your mind, emotions, and flesh who seek to make your life miserable and destroy you. The fallen demonic realm's main objective is to keep you from finding the "one thing." However, God has also enabled his angels and the Holy Spirit to come to us, speak to us, and comfort us as we work our way through the trials of living separate from God.

Your ability to know the difference between the voices in this realm will come from being able to discern the subtle differences between the two. Once you can come to a place where you are filled with the Holy Spirit, where your spirit is awakened, you will develop the gift of discernment which is imparted to you freely. This tool is invaluable in understanding whether the voices that come into your thought process have your overall best interest or just seem so on the surface but ultimately lead to your demise. I will tell you this from my experience: The voices from heaven are designed to lead you back to your identity in God and bridge the gap that keeps you separate from him. All other voices that feed yourself or condemn you, whether human or spirit, are demonic in origin. These are the voices that have their origination from the tree of knowledge.

The authority over the fallen atmosphere was originally given to man, but after the fall it was then given over to Satan and the angels that fell with him. It is seen in the spirit as a thick cloud barrier or pall that blocks the sun and keeps us, so to speak, in the dark and separate from the light. It is in the light that our eyes are open and we begin to see clearly. I will explain how to walk in light in the proceeding chapters. Your ability to differentiate the two natures will come from your ability to see. Sight or vision will come from the amount of light you are able to walk in. Your spirit is capable of knowing the differences between the two. Your carnal nature is not! Therefore, you must do all you can to put your spirit in the place where it can open up to see. To do this you will need to obtain the knowledge and vision that will lead to wisdom.

In the next chapter, "The Seven Steps," I will talk about the tabernacle of God. There are seven steps and also three levels, which are the outer court, the inner court, and the Most Holy Place. Our whole journey from hereon will be going from outer to inner. The outer court represents the first realm while the inner court represents the second realm.

The second heaven is the pass-through realm which is also known as the veil of separation that keeps us from the "one thing." Once you know how to pass through and get to the other side, you will find the secret of your life. People who have died and come back report seeing themselves passing through a dark tunnel moving toward a light, and when they get through the tunnel, they are in heaven. What they are experiencing is passing through the second heaven. Our goal is to enter the third realm, which is the place where you will find the "one thing." In my previous book, *To the Ends of the Earth*, in part 2, "Ascending the Mountain," I have written more in depth on the three heavens. It is not my focus here to spend too much time on this subject.

The third realm, also known as the third heaven, is a much talked about and elusive place that has fascinated mankind since the beginning of time. This is the place we will travel to, and the destination where you will find the "one thing." I will only tell you this about the third heaven—once you taste what it has to offer, you will never be the same. The rest of this book will be devoted to how to enter and walk in the place you were created to.

Before we move on, I want to give you the access route to the third heaven. This is the Biblical secret of finding your way to and into the place where you were designed to live.

> The earth is the Lord's and everything in it, the world, and all who live in it; for he founded it upon the seas and established it upon the waters.
>
> Who may ascend the hill of the Lord?
>
> Who may stand in his holy place?
>
> He who has clean hands and a pure heart, who does not lift up his soul to an idol or swear by what is false.
>
> He will receive blessing from the Lord and vindication from God his Savior.
>
> Such is the generation of those who seek him, who seek your face, O God of Jacob."
>
> Lift up your heads, O you gates; be lifted up, you ancient doors, that the King of glory may come in.
>
> Psalms 24:1–7 (NIV)

To enter the third realm, you have to come to a place where you can learn to walk in your new redeemed nature in the spirit. Once you do, you may ascend the hill of God and enter the gates of heaven and his holy place. When you learn what the seven steps are and how to take them, then you will be able to enter and walk in this realm.

The desert and the parched land will be glad; the wilderness will rejoice and blossom.

Like the crocus it will burst into bloom;
it will rejoice greatly and shout for joy.
The glory of Lebanon will be given to it,
the splendor of Carmel and Sharon;
they will see the glory of the Lord, the splendor of our God.

Strengthen the feeble hands, steady the knees that give way; say to those with fearful hearts, "Be strong, do not fear; your God will come, he will come with vengeance; with divine retribution he will come to save you.

Then the eyes of the blind will be opened and the ears of the deaf unstopped.

Then will the lame leap like a deer, and the mute tongue shout for joy.

Water will gush forth in the wilderness and streams in the desert.

The burning sand will become a pool, the thirsty ground bubbling springs.

In the haunts where jackals once lay, grass and reeds and papyrus will grow.

And a highway will be there; it will be called the Way of Holiness.

The unclean will not journey on it; it will be for those that walk in that Way; wicked fools will not go about on it.

No lion will be there, nor will any ferocious beast get up on it; they will not be found there.

But only the redeemed will walk there, and the ransomed of the Lord will return.

> They will enter Zion with singing; everlasting
> joy will crown their heads.
>   Gladness and joy will overtake them, and
> sorrow and sighing will flee away.
>
> Isaiah 35: 1-10

Once you get a grip on what I am laying out for you here, life will come back to the dryness you now live in, and all your senses will come alive. You will see the highway of holiness and be able to walk on it with your created nature, your spirit man. Your beast nature will no longer be a factor as it needs to be laid to rest to get on the *way*. Part of the secret is to learn to park that old nature on the side of the road. Once you learn to walk on it, you will enter the third heaven and experience things you never imagined before. Your spirit will come alive and you will be able to leap and bound into the heights of God while all your senses will open up so you can see and hear God.

> There is a mine for silver and a place where gold
> is refined.
>   Iron is taken from the earth, and copper is
> smelted from ore.
>   Man puts an end to the darkness; he searches
> the farthest recesses for ore in the blackest
> darkness.
>   Far from where people dwell he cuts a shaft
> in the places forgotten by the foot of man; for
> from men he dangles and sways.
>   The earth from which food comes, is
> transformed below as by fire; sapphires come

from its rocks and its dust contains nuggets of gold.

No bird of prey knows that hidden path, no falcon's eye has seen it.

Proud beasts do not set foot on it and no lion prowls there.

Job 28: 1–8

It is by turning from your outer man to your inner man, getting into a meditative state where you can transition to your spirit and leave your beast behind, where you can cut a shaft through the second heaven and enter the third. Once you do, the gates of heaven are open for you to enter and discover the "one thing."

One thing to note is that the way into the third realm is not some small path but a highway. It is also not a one-way street. Any highway I have seen has multiple lanes going in both directions. It is built for mass transit to and from heaven. Once we learn to travel on this highway and enter the third heaven, we understand things on a whole new level. Our perspective is more vast, where we can get a much better understanding about the issues surrounding our lives that we live with every day in the low places. Aside from making sense of our lives, your heavenly Father also gives you creative ideas to improve the world you live in. The idea is to travel freely and unencumbered up to heaven, receive what you will from God, and then take it back down to earth where you can learn to apply it. It is important to understand that a highway is a two-way street.

One final thought before we move on: When you read your Bible, you are doing so with your intellect, thus feeding your soul. The written word of God is foundational, like a launching pad, which will give you what you need to ascend into the heights in God. Whenever you do anything in the natural, emotional, or spiritual in the first or second realms, you are feeding your soul and intellect. It is only when you ascend into the third heaven and learn to rest there that you will truly feed your spirit and experience the living word of God which has relevance for today.

THE SEVEN STEPS

The blueprint for how your life was designed to be lived.

The steps will lead you to the place where you can find rest and healing. It is a return to your original DNA. Once understood, these seven steps are so simple that anyone can enter the realm of the "one thing" in the blink of an eye.

It's really going to get exciting from hereon, and I hope by now you are looking forward to all the possibilities your heart is crying out for. It is at this point you will either turn around and call it quits as you listen to those voices that have limited you in the past, or your desire to know more of the truth about yourself will push you past all fears and limitations. During each of the seven steps, you will have to adjust your thought process, changing from old, rigid patterns so you can be increasingly transformed through each step. You will be challenged at each step and will have to make a fateful decision to trust what lies ahead and take a chance, or return to where you came from settling for your old ways. Each step builds upon each other. They are designed in their specific order to bring you to completion. The Author and Creator of the universe mapped out these profoundly easy steps to the throne of grace and to the restoration of who you truly are.

I hope by now that your carnal mind has marinated long enough for that thick, dense skull to be cracked open so your thoughts can be set free enough to explore the possibilities of all you ever hoped for and desired for your life. You may be one who has never taken any of these steps, for the many reasons you have had, to this point, and I would encourage you to push past your logic to see where these seven steps will lead. Some of you may already have some of these steps in place in you lives, while some may have figured out most of them, but all seven are needed to complete the journey. Our goal is the "one thing"—for you to discover the secret to your life—and that is at the seventh step.

In the Bible, God gave Moses a blueprint on how a fallen man can approach him, how to get past the bouncer at the gate with the flaming sword. In this case, it's not who you know, but *what* you know that will get you in. It is called the *tabernacle*. In this blueprint, there are three levels and seven steps. The three levels coincide with the three realms and they are called the *outer court*, the *inner court* and the *Most Holy Place*. The Most Holy Place is the place in the tabernacle where the presence of God dwelt and was blocked by a thick curtain called the *veil of separation*. Man was not allowed to go beyond the curtain in his uncircumcised state or in his fallen nature, or else he would be smoked. Nothing dirty can come before God, or the glory of his presence will burn it. The high priest, as part of his duty, was to go beyond the veil and maintain the Most Holy Place. The other priests would tie a rope around his waist, and if it went slack for a long time, they knew he wasn't clean before he went in, and he was toasted. They had to drag his dead body out. So now, the priesthood had to find someone else to be appointed high priest to go in and suffer the same fate if their hearts weren't right and their egos were too huge. How would you like that job?

The seven steps are designed to lead you through each level and actually prepare you to be a high priest that can enter the Most Holy Place and be in the glory of his presence without fear of dying. I will lay this out for you and show you God's design to restore you to the way you were originally created—to have a relationship with him, to walk with him in the cool breeze of the day, experiencing his perfect love, and enjoying all the trees of the garden that you were meant to eat from. However, to get to this place, your biggest obstacle is unlearning everything from the tree of knowledge of good and evil and shrinking the cranium. If you had a choice of only good, or both good and bad, what would you choose? One is simple while the other choice is complicated. There are two choices, only good, in which all you have to do is enjoy the atmosphere God created for you and bask in the purity of all its qualities, or both good and bad, where you have to try to figure out like some huge jigsaw puzzle without a picture what your life is about. There is nothing behind door three.

If you choose "only good," then you will need to understand the seven steps and how to approach God with your higher nature and temporarily park on the side your fallen nature. I will show you how to get glimpses into heaven right now; as I said, you don't have to wait to die physically. Imagine that! If you are ready, let me begin to unfold and explain how this blueprint works. As in the Rubik's Cube, the secret in solving it is understanding its access and pivot point and all the other steps that revolve around it. The secret of the Bible in its message to fallen man is the hope of restored relationship with God by knowing the spiritual access and pivot points and how our lives revolve around it. If you don't know this, you are trying to figure out the jigsaw puzzle without the picture. No matter how much time you spend reading the Bible, or any other books, is futile. You just keep spinning the sides of the cube and the colors never line up. But once you do, then solving it becomes exponentially easier.

The tabernacle was, and is, designed for all God's people to come worship him at the level of their comfort. Aside from the three courts in the temple, everyone has to start from outside the walls of the temple and enter the gate. The first step is entering the gate, which is called the gate of salvation. If you were unwilling to enter this gate, then your whole experience and belief structure of God was from outside the tabernacle. Your understanding of God was at a great distance, and most of what you believed was from what others told you or you read about. You were relegated to believe in what man told you. Your belief structure was wrapped in listening to a fallen man and hearsay, not firsthand experience.

Many on the outside, because of their unwillingness to enter, created their own view on God from that vantage point, and thus the many religions were created—God, in our image, to accomplish what we want. There are many religions also in the outer and inner courts as well. Man has a way of making a religion at each step except the seventh step. The problem with all religions is they further separate people from each other and God. Many come in the name of God, but few know God. There is no need for religion at the seventh step, because everything man made had to fall away in order to approach the seventh step. As I said before, each step is sequential; and in order to get to the seventh step, you must not stop at any other step and make a religion out of it.

Please understand that I didn't design this pattern, nor do I want to create my own religion. I just want to show you God's design that you can accept or reject. Many have asked what makes one religion think they have the answer over another. Each religion has a portion of the truth, whether they worship God from outside the gates, in the outer court or the inner court, but none has the whole truth until they enter the Most Holy Place. My goal is not to tell you what you believe is right or wrong, but to allow you to see it for yourself, expand on what you believe, and bring you all the way home. I hope to answer some of the questions here about the many religions and why they are what they are without writing another book. I will be brief because I want to stay focused on the "one thing." I could also write a chapter on each of these steps, but again I want to be expedient and stay on point.

Step 1

The gates of salvation represented the promise by God to send a savior, which he did, and whom most of the Jews and the world rejected. What separates most religions from the one God designed is *Jesus*. Jesus is the savior, and he is the gate into the tabernacle, a place all of us can enter and experience God in a more personal and deeper way. I am not saying that your belief in God is wrong. If you don't accept Jesus as your Lord and Savior, it is just from a distance and outside the tabernacle. It is limited. You need to take this first step to enter. This is your first choice at your first step to the secret of life and the "one thing." Do you want only good or both good and bad? You must take this step to go on; there is no other way! All the arguments in the world can't change what God designed—either accept it or reject it. You have nothing to lose and everything to gain if you accept it and enter.

Jesus said, "I am the way, the truth and the life and no one comes to the Father except through me." He also said, "It is through me and not to me that you will gain access into the Kingdom of Heaven." Jesus is the first step, the gate of salvation, which opens up the rest of the tabernacle experience that allows you to take the next six steps. It is also a place you enter with thanksgiving. "Enter His gates with thanksgiving and His courts with praise" Psalm 100:4 (NIV).

It is at the first step and gate of salvation that many people stop and form other religions, which I would call salvation or evangelical churches, and their total focus is getting people saved. This is not God's intent or the end of his plan. This is only the first step in the ongoing process of salvation. His plan is for complete restoration of your mind, body, soul, and spirit. You can't stop here and make a religion, or you will miss the glory of God. If you do, it's another man-made creation. The first step is only the access point and the pivot point which everything revolves around and the first level of the secret to solving the cube of your live. God is the goal; Jesus is the way.

Step 2

Once you take the first step and enter the outer court, there are two pieces of furniture which represent the next two steps. They are the bronze altar or altar of burnt offerings and the basin or laver. As you enter the tabernacle, the first place you would stop, and the second step, is the bronze altar. This was the place where you would offer the best of your herd or crop. It is also known as the place of offering and sacrifice. You would take your biggest and strongest bull, and the priests would sacrifice it and then make a burnt offering unto God. It is the place where the beast was put to death. It is now symbolic to its original intent and material sacrifice is not required. That was done by Jesus through his death on the cross which paid for all our debts. The second step is also the place of the cross for us to hang our old coat on so we can be cleansed in the next step and made ready for our new garment at the fourth step.

This is the place where God wants your best, which is not you money or things. He wants you to sacrifice the beast within you, put it on the altar to be put to death and turned into a burnt offering unto him. That beast is the old nature, your intellect, that was born in the garden after the fall of man and separated from God. It is overcoming self! It is here God wants you to learn to make still your old ways and allow your spirit to rise up and walk with him. This is the place of repentance where you turn from your fallen nature, where your created nature can be cleaned, nourished, opened up, and be made ready to pass through the veil and visit with him. It is also the place where you smash the cranium and crush your intellect. Your intellect is the beast.

Many religions are born here where their focus is on repentance or a harsh treatment of the flesh. They create an idol of the cross in which their final destination is the cross, instead of using it as a gateway through which you can grow into spiritual maturity. The cross is nothing more than a coat hanger where you hang your old garment so you can move on free of its weight.

STEP 3

The next step is the laver or basin, which represents cleansing with water. It is a washing clean of the old nature after it has been sacrificed on the altar. The basin also represents water baptism, which is also symbolic of burying the old nature in water while the new nature emerges clean. As you emerge cleansed and renewed you are ready to understand the word of God to retrain your thinking. When your spirit is awakened, it is much easier to understand the words of the Bible through the Holy Spirit it was written in. The words seem to come alive and jump off the pages when you read it through your spiritual mind.

The Bible was written by people who learned to operate in the third realm. It is called the realm of eagles; those who had their eyes and ears wide open and were able to scroll down what God was speaking at the time, with as little of their own self in the way of his original intent. When we get into the third level, you will see how the prophets operate and how you can learn to be an eagle and soar into the heights on God's breath. This will also dispel the argument that the Bible was written by mere men. Yes, it was written by men, but not fallen men. They were walking in their spirits with God in the realm that was rarified and pure. There wasn't any self nature in the way of what God said.

It is here as well where many other church types, which totally focus on water baptism or the word of God, are born. The Baptist church believes that if you are not water baptized, you can't get filled with the Spirit, and some go on to believe you are not even saved. The so-called word churches stop at the Bible, and they make an idol out of it. They make you like perpetual ground school students; they use their knowledge of the Bible to control other students but never allow what it says to put them to flight. The Bible can be, and has been used as, a very powerful weapon to control others and accommodate what man wants to create. We must be careful to allow the words to set us free and not create another bondage to hold us back.

At any station along the way, we can stop and build a religion which will prevent us from going all the way and completing the journey. Each and every step is important, and I am not diminishing any of them, but they are steps which lead upwards to the throne of God. Everything so far has been in the first realm where the outer court religions and churches exist and thus limit their people from going into the next realm or inner court. The three steps in the outer court are meant to prepare you for what is inside the inner court. The first three steps are salvation, repentance, and cleansing.

Now we will go from the outer to the inner. In the Old Testament times, only the Levitical priesthood could enter the inner court of the physical temple of the tabernacle. That temple has long been destroyed, but the temple I am talking about is you. You are the temple of God, whether you want to believe it or not. God dwells inside you in your spirit. For many, their spirits have been so suppressed for so long the recognition of this side of themselves is diminished. Through Jesus, repentance, and cleansing, we are made ready to be the priesthood, and we are now allowed to enter the inner court. No beast is allowed inside the temple of God; they must remain on the outside.

Before we go in, I want to stop a moment and talk about why most religions, churches, and ministries fear going inside the temple. It is because there is a cost, the dying of your old nature. Most feel comfortable in maintaining their fallen nature by feeding their spirit with an outer court or first realm understanding of the things of God. This is why they create superficial religions. They also fear the unknown, nor do they want to deal with the messes they might encounter going inside the temple. If you are unwilling to overcome what happened to you at the tree of knowledge and deal with it, your whole experience will be from the outside. What's even worse, if you are unwilling to go further, you will try to justify your position and attack everyone who is willing to go beyond where you are. This is a main reason why religion is so ugly and a major limitation to people finding the fullness of God. It is here at this point you and only you can decide if you want to go in and get deeper with God.

Many will condemn what goes on in the inside of the temple due to their unwillingness to enter, while others will feel too unworthy to enter and will allow the voices of others to stop them. This is why it is crucial for you to lay down your old nature, with all its limitations, at the bronze altar. If you are able, you will easily make the transition to the nature that is excited about what lies ahead and not care about what lies behind. Don't look back, it will freeze you; look forward and you will find your secret. You will be free to enter, and nothing can hold you back.

As you enter the inner court, you will see three pieces of furniture and see the veil which separates man from God. The inner court represents the second realm of heaven. The three pieces of furniture are the table of showbread, the lamp stand and the altar of incense.

With each step you take and realm you enter, you are getting closer to not only God, but the "one thing." His presence also grows increasingly stronger as you near the glory realm of God, the place where everything will clear up.

STEP 4

The first place you will stop, and fourth step, is the table of showbread, also known as the bread of his presence. This is where you will learn to have communion with your Father and understand its true meaning. As you eat of the bread and ingest it, your spirit is being fed from God. You are suddenly awakened as your spiritual senses burst forth with new life. There is a new vibrancy as your inner man is brought out of the dark. This is where you meet the Holy Spirit or are baptized in the Spirit. It is called the "born again experience." You were born of the flesh on your birth date, which is your natural birth. You are born of the spirit when the Holy Spirit enters your heart, thus you are born again. If you have not taken this step, I would highly encourage you to let go and abandon your old way of thinking because your heart will experience a level of love you had no idea existed before. You will absolutely experience incredible feelings and find freedoms that weren't possible before. As Jesus is the gateway into the tabernacle, the Holy Spirit is the gateway into the temple and inner court and the beginning of having communion with God.

It is at this step where most of the charismatic, Pentecostal, and born-again churches build their religions. Even though they have gone further along the path to God than most they stopped at the fourth step and ended their journey. I will say it is better to stop inside the temple than somewhere on the outside as your relationship with God has gotten so much deeper and better. However, you have still fallen short of the "one thing."

It's getting intense now, and I hope your level of excitement is growing as we near the end of the journey. Not many people go this far. Most have made camp somewhere along the journey and decided they have gone far enough. They are satisfied with the portion of the truth they have found. If you are a Jonathan Livingston Seagull, you will not settle for anything less than the fullness you can achieve if you push on. I myself have stopped many times along the way, but when discontentment set in and I listened to the voice that told me there was more, I rose up and started walking again until I found the place of fulfillment. This is why I write this for you, to show you what I have seen and found and leave it up to you to decide what truths you want to take from this.

STEP 5

The fifth step is at the lamp stand with seven candles. This is the place of illumination where your eyes and ears are opened to perceive the voice of God more clearly than at any previous step. This is the place of revelation where the prophetic giftings are giving to those that stand before the lamp stand. There are three candles on one side and three on the other, with one in the middle. Three candles represent the first three steps in the outer court, while the other three represent the three steps on the inner court. The candle in the middle represents the seventh and final step. Each candle gives illumination for the coinciding step, giving you insight and revelation while you are at that step about the things of God. The more candles you collect, the brighter things get. When you get to seven lumens, or illuminations, you are in the glory realm of God.

It's at this step, as you visit the lamp stand over and over again, that your spiritual senses will deepen. The fog covering your eyes will start to dissipate, and your vision will sharpen. The once-faint voices of heaven will clear up and become more distinct. Your ability to discern the differences between the three voices will also grow. In order to understand and learn revelation, you have to be at the place of revelation. It is here the gifts of the Holy Spirit will also be developed. This is the staging area where eagles learn to fly to prepare themselves for flight. Your spirit is growing stronger with each visit as all your senses are deepening and your perceptions are clearing up. It is from here you will unfold your wings, mount up on wings of eagles, and soar into the heights of God on his breath.

Those who stop here at this step build their prophetic ministries and use their giftings to lead others into their own creations leading many astray. Many of these prophetic ministries want to look good before men, to be recognized by men and also to make money. They are no different than the money changers that Jesus kicked out of God's temple. A true prophet speaks for God without any need for recognition or gain. If it does come, he knows how to deal and process it and keep his relationship with God in the right order. Many good men and women falter at this level because they lose sight of what got them here.

STEP 6

Each step so far has been designed to prepare you for the sixth step which you take at the altar of incense. It is the place of ascension where you will climb into the third realm and enter the third heaven, the very place where God dwells. At the alter of incense, the priest would light the physical body of the incense which would burn releasing a vapor and fragrance going upwards. The hard body, as it burned, turned to ash and fell away. Here you leave everything behind and become a vapor to rising up becoming a sweet aroma to God's nostrils.

It is the launching pad, and when the match is lit, we have ignition and we take off into the heights. It is here you rend the mind and bring stillness to your old thoughts and ways of thinking. "Be still and know I am the Lord your God." Psalm 46:10 (NIV). From here your spiritual mind is able to soar into the heights with God. There is nothing left to hold you back now. This is where you learn to ascend Mount Zion, the holy mountain of God, and push past the veil of separation and come to the seventh step. If you wanted to climb a mountain, you would make all your preparations travel to it and then ascend to get to the top. You wouldn't camp out and look at the mountain, read about it, or admire it. Your purpose is to assault the heights and the only way to do it is to ascend. The three steps you take in the inner Court are *infilling*, *illumination* and *ascension*. Ascension leads to the seventh step.

This is the place where some who get this far build their monasteries and live on the heights alone and separate from people and the fallen world. These religions want to live their lives in the quiet places with God, separated from mankind, avoiding all the turmoil that assaults our spiritual nature in the low places. I will tell you the problem with this at a later time.

Step 7

You are at the veil of separation which you need to penetrate to enter into the third realm. "You are about to enter the no-sin zone." You can not go beyond the veil of separation with your sin nature—fallen nature—present. The cherubim with the flaming sword will stop you for your own good. You have to lay it down on the altar of burnt offerings. It's wiser to let it burn on the bronze altar which was designed to offer your old nature than to be so arrogant to think you can come before God with it intact. If you think the fire at the altar is hot, you have no idea how hot it can get in the glory realm of God. To enter this atmosphere, you want to be humble and covered with the Holy Spirit, dressed in your new white robe.

The high priest, who was able to enter the Most Holy Place where the presence of God was intense, had to be the most humble man amongst the bunch. It wasn't a position for the person with the most titles or degrees. It was not a place for the person with the largest intellect either. It was a place for the simple, the people with child-like faith, the headless and pure of heart, which is humility. I don't approach God and give him my resume or tell him who I am. He sees past the facade I try to create for myself and directly into my heart. He knows me better than I may think, as he created me and my spiritual nature. It is my own creation of the beast nature I need to leave behind as I enter this most magnificent place and walk in the nature that was designed to be here. If you can learn this one simple thing and flip the switch, you can enter and discover the "one thing."

I will put in a nutshell what sin is so you don't have to spend your whole life trying to figure it out. It's so simple it will blow your mind. Here it is: *It is separation from God!* Everything else we do is a result of separation. Again, it is by the tree we eat of that we feed either the created nature or the sin nature. When I am separated from God, which is any step below the seventh step, I am eating of the wrong tree and feeding the wrong nature. All other steps lead to the seventh step and place of rest. It is at the seventh step I can rest from living in my fallen nature and be at peace with the creation. I tell you, I tell you, *I tell you,* you have to really let go and abandon your old ways to experience what I am telling you about here. Humility is abandonment of your individual self. This is what the Bible means when it says "to walk in the Spirit." *Your spirit with God's Spirit,* not speaking in tongues, or prophecy, or any other gift of the Spirit. Plain and simple! Don't try to reason or argue. It won't work before God. It is a place to just be and absorb. "To be or not to be is the question." The "one thing" is the atmosphere of love we are entitled to walk in.

It is at this point we have to enter completely, devoid of our own identity, having nailed it to the cross. We strip away our old dirty garments in the first six steps and put on our white robe—the robe of righteousness—the covering of the Holy Spirit which enables our created nature to come alive and walk spirit to spirit with God. This is the place where our spirits can be fed from the tree of life. No one can fully understand how to fulfill the first commandment until you enter the third realm and love God from this place. Attempting to love God from our brokenness is a mere shadow of loving him from the fullness we are capable of. Once you can grasp this one truth, you are now ready to understand what the "one thing" is.

As you enter the Most Holy Place, there is only one piece of furniture, and that is the ark of the covenant. It represents the place of the power of God in the midst of man. Since the destruction of the temple and disappearance of the ark, this place represents our ascension into the third heaven and holy mountain of God. It is here we can enter the gates of heaven and can walk in the original creation, experiencing all it has to offer. You don't have to wait to die and wonder if you will make it. You can enter it now and have glimpses into heaven while you are alive on earth. If you can learn to make this transition, you are standing at the doorway to knowing the "one thing." In the next chapter, you will learn how to rest in this place and get to know the "one thing."

To summarize, here are the seven steps in order: salvation, repentance, baptism, infilling, illumination, ascension, and rest. The goal is *rest*! Once you understand the significance of each step and how to take it, you can be at the place of rest in a flash.

The "One Thing"

Your quest for the secret of life is answered. Once you find the place of the "one thing," you can understand what it is you have been looking for your whole life, and you will find the answers you have long sought. It is here. All the mysteries of your life will unfold, and the truth will be revealed.

"You will work for six days, and on the seventh day you will rest." This is a biblical concept to what is called *Sabbath rest*. It is in the third realm that you can truly grasp this concept. It also parallels the first six steps in the tabernacle. Once you get to the seventh step, it is the place where you rest at the throne of God. Yes, you get to not only visit and experience the glory of God up close and personal, but you learn to rest in it absorbing all the good qualities by just being in the atmosphere of perfection. If you want to be holy, then you need to be in the atmosphere of holiness. There is no other way—not by how many books you read, how religious you are in your ideology, or how pious you try to be on earth.

The secret to life and the "one thing" is learning to walk with God, not separate from him. You have to know how to walk with God spirit to spirit and see him face to face. You need to overcome your separation from him, living in a fallen world, in your fallen nature. It is about your restored relationship with your Heavenly Father and learning to walk in his creation. It is about entering the gates of heaven now and experiencing all that heaven has to offer. The gates of heaven are symbolic of penetrating the veil and entering the Most Holy Place. Psalm 100:4 NIV says, "To enter his gates with thanksgiving and his courts with praise." It is a condition of the heart in which we enter, and not just a belief structure. You can't enter by just believing or thinking about it; you have to rise up in your spirit with your heart right and enter.

It is kind of ironic that at this juncture, while I was writing this book, I received an e-mail that summarized everything I am saying here. It was beyond ironic; it was actually God speaking to me at this point in the book and pouring out more revelation. Most of this book is written through direct revelation from God backed up by my experiences in the third heaven. Once you learn how to hear and see the voice of God, you will understand the many ways he can communicate with you. The e-mail was combined with beautiful photos, and it said that the shortest chapter in the Bible is Psalms 117 and the longest is 119. The chapter that is in the center of the Bible is Psalms 118 and that there are 594 chapters before and after this one, which add up to 1188 chapters. Then it goes on to say the center verse in the Bible is Psalms 118:8. The NIV version of the Bible says, "It is better to take refuge in the Lord than to trust man." Bingo! You have the "one thing" in a nutshell. God's ways just blow me away. The center of the Bible is the key pivot point and secret to life, just like the Rubik's cube. Yes, six sides all matching in color, and then you lay it down complete and take rest. Just literally amazing! How do you take refuge? You enter his house. The seventh step is all about entering his house and taking refuge in him.

"My desire is to dwell in the house of the Lord," Psalms 23:6 (NIV). You can start now!

You want to know what faith is. Your faith is developed as your spirit is developed. It is hard to walk in faith when your spirit is atrophied and weak. As you spend more and more time walking with God in this realm, your spirit strengthens and your level of faith grows. Faith is spiritual strength! You cannot develop the level of faith you can have on the other side of the veil of separation. It is marginal at best. You can say you believe in faith or even go as far as to think you have faith, but until you cross the threshold and enter the third heaven, you have no idea what faith is. Faith is developed by resting in the atmosphere of heaven.

Jesus said, "The kingdom of heaven is at hand." That means the atmosphere of this spiritual kingdom surrounds us. It is present and can be seen as easily as the natural kingdom or first heaven. You don't need to plan a trip and travel some great distance to get there. It is right in front of your face, and once you enter, you will learn to open up to it and walk in it. It is accessed through the seven steps by understanding how to break through the veil of separation in your mind and letting your spirit free. Once you understand the "one thing" and learn to walk in it, it will be natural for you to make the transition. You can enter the kingdom of heaven at a moment's notice. All you do is set your focus on things above, leave all your worries behind, ascend and enter.

Once you enter this place and you can rest in it, everything you once thought was important will no longer matter while you are there. You will come to realize all your religion, philosophical beliefs, and everything you thought was valuable in the natural world will be a mere shadow of what it seemed in the light of God. It will all seem so irrelevant during your visits. You will also attain new priorities for your life on earth as old patterns fall by the wayside. With each visit, you grow by feeding your created nature from the tree of life. Your spirit strengthens as well as your level of faith.

The level of love in this place is so overwhelming and consuming you will realize that the best moment of love on earth is conditional and limited. All you get is conditional love on the south side of the veil. Once you penetrate this barrier, all you will find is unconditional love. You are free to take as much as your vessel will carry. At first, your heart will seem like a colander, full of holes, and incapable of keeping this kind of love for long. After your visit, when you walk back in the natural atmosphere, it seems to dissipate rather quickly; but as you frequent the "one thing," the less porous your vessel becomes. One day you will be able to retain enough of God's unconditional love to pour out on others.

Children are like love sponges seeking unconditional love. They also will absorb anything else we put in them. Usually, at best we give them conditional love, but often it's not love at all. We wonder why our children grow up all messed up, or they too closely resemble us—all the bad qualities we hate. It is why Jesus said it is easier for a child to enter heaven than the wise and prudent. The heart of a child just desires pure love that is why we need to return to this simple attitude. Unconditional love is found in the heart and presence of God. It is here we can soak up all the love we need and in time develop the capability to love others unconditionally as we are loved. The best of us, without experiencing this kind of love, were unable to give the love we need to others. The more brokenness we have, the greater the conditions become in our lack to love others. It is in being in the atmosphere of love that we not only are healed, but we become more socially functional and can make a difference in our community.

Let me define the "one thing" again, in case you haven't understood it by now. It is not just believing in God, but knowing how to have a relationship with him in the place he created for us as we walk and talk with him, being his friend in the garden. The secret is a place and position. Through taking all seven steps, you have access to the realm of God. It is finding that perfect place within yourself and learning how to position yourself before God that will allow you to rest in the purity of God's creation. It is like being in a bubble of isolation from all the problems of the world for the time of your visitation.

Your beliefs, your religion, or even doing the work of God will not bring you before the throne of God. Nor will reading books about him, even the Bible. No, it's something much more profound that goes beyond the pages and words. Those are still external practices which keep our mind active. It is bringing your mind to total rest that will open the door to heaven. Then all you have to do is love God in his house. Yes, it is that simple. The "one thing" is the first commandment! It is the only commandment we need to focus on. There is no need to worry about any other command, because we can't fulfill any of them without getting this one right. Men make religions out of the last nine commandments.

It is learning to love God beyond our conditional love that we are capable of in our fallen nature and transitioning to our spiritual nature where we can love and walk with God the way we should. The first commandment goes way beyond what appears on the surface of loving God above all else. Yes, it is above all else, and that means all the activity of the world we live in. It is finding that place where you can position yourself to have no other focus but being with him, no other thought than being in a relationship with your Creator. It is a state of being, where everything else in your world disappears for that moment in time you are with him. It is walking in perfection where there is only good, where all the negative thoughts you live with in the world have fallen by the wayside for the time being. The "one thing" is being in the atmosphere where you can be transformed by nothing more than being there and walking in it. All the work comes in the first six steps. Once you arrive at the seventh step, you rest and enjoy.

You will also come to realize that the very religion or practice you believed was designed to bring you closer to God was actually keeping you away from him. Most of your experience was worshipping God from afar. I am not saying religion is bad; it will just limit your relationship with God, unless that practice focuses on the first commandment and leads you to him. The more you walk with God, the more you will see the limitations to man's ways. Most of men's ways focus on your fallen nature, causing you to worry about the wrong thing and what's wrong with you. God's way is designed for you to focus on your created nature being in his presence of his love, allowing transformation to come by atmosphere and not work.

We must learn to make the transition from your outer man to your inward man, to be still and shut down all the external stimuli. Psalms 37:7 NIV says, "Be still before the Lord and wait patiently for him…" It is in the posturing of stillness of your outer man that the revelation and glory of God will happen. Psalms 46:10 NIV says, "Be still and know that I am God." Once we make the transition into the place of external stillness, the kingdom of God opens up and we get caught up to the third heaven. It is here we come to know God. This is the secret to the "one thing" and the access point. Stillness!

In this atmosphere as we reflect on his perfect love we are transformed. "For we know in part and we prophecy in part, but when perfection comes the imperfect disappears." "Now we see but a poor reflection as in a mirror, dimly lit, then we shall see face to face. Now I know in part; then I shall know fully, even as I am fully known," I Corinthians 13:9 and 12 (NIV). In the quiet place clarity opens up, what once seemed vague and dim becomes more in focus with each visit with him. The secret, again, is being in the place of perfection where all the problems and mysteries of your life can be cleared up and you are made whole. The "one thing" is learning to walk in this way.

Let me ask you a question. Do you love someone by listening to others about them, reading about them, looking at pictures of them? Or do you find out where they are and want be with them? I think everyone of us to a tee will do the latter. If we love someone, we do all we can to spend as much time as possible with them. We want to walk and talk and even enjoy resting in each other's arms in an embrace. With God, perhaps because he seems so far off or inanimate and untouchable, you have not known how to love him in this way. There are people throughout history, probably few and far between, who have known the way to approach God and love him where he dwells. Where does God dwell? In the third heaven! How can we love God? We have to enter the realm he dwells in. The "one thing" is also about entering the gates of heaven as well as walking in that realm.

THE "ONE THING"

There are a few people who really stand out to me in the Bible, who learned to walk in this way, but there's one in particular whose whole story is summed up in a few sentences. His name in Enoch, and he found a way to crack the code and get past the angels with the flaming sword, walk with God, and love him in his house. His epitaph reads, "He walked with God for three hundred years, and he was not." In other words, he loved God so much that he spent as much time with him as he could. The more time he did, the less his fallen nature controlled him until it was gone. He was taken up to heaven without facing death. Is that possible for you? You bet it is. Enoch knew to enter God's realm. He had to take the seven steps and lay down his old nature while he was with God.

There are also many who got caught up into the third heaven and had visitations in the glory realm of God. I would say most if not all the authors of the Bible have had these experiences as well as the mystics and people who live in monasteries. I have been caught up many times. But that is not what the "one thing" is about. It is not about you waiting and hoping someday the clouds will part and a glory beam of light will descend upon you and you will be caught up. The difference is about you knowing the secret path to access heaven whenever you want, just like Enoch and a few others did. If your passion for a person is strong enough, you will find a way around all obstacles and seek them out until you find them. Once you do, nothing can stop you. The only thing that can stop you from this place is yourself and your lack of knowledge of how to walk in the way, on the highway of holiness to be in God's face.

I could write volumes about my experiences with being in the atmosphere of heaven, but it is not my intention to tell you what I saw. It is my intention to show you the "one thing" so you yourself can go have your own experiences, to see all the majestic and glorious views of this place. Why listen to my story when you can have your own? I truly hope that you will push all your busyness aside, find a quiet place, and take the time in your life so you can begin to seek out the things I have written here for you. It will take a time investment on your part and a sacrifice of old ways to embark on this journey, but it will be well worth it once you arrive and find God in his creation.

It is written that "People perish for a lack of knowledge." No one has ever told you about the "one thing," the secret to understanding your life and solving your cube. You are dying on earth and slowly perishing because you have not known how to approach God and walk with him. The knowledge of his pathways is sourced from the tree of life. I have walked with God for many years, staring into his face through which he has shown me the secret path to him and how to apply it to my daily life. I hope to show you in simple terms without complicating the way for you to find it for yourself. I hope, if nothing else, I have made this simple enough for you to follow it so you can find it for yourself.

HOW TO APPLY
IT TO YOUR LIFE

How to apply the secret to your life here on Earth so you can enjoy the peace and joy you always desired. Understanding the concept of it is one thing, but applying it is another.

The battle over your mind will start the moment you try to slow your thought process down so you can find a quiet place and time. All the forces and impulses from your outer self will wage against your thought process. The battle over middle earth begins! Sounds like a *Lord of the Rings* line, but it is between your lower and higher nature which is your mind. The better you can prepare for this, the easier it will be to make the transition from the lowlands to the highlands.

You are going to have to accept a few things, if you haven't already, in order to make it work for you. I did not create the Rubik's Cube, nor did I create you and the world we all live in. I am only a messenger who found the secret of life and the "one thing." I, daily, am learning to apply it to my life. It is not a one-time or once in a while thing. We are all fighting some very strong forces that are trying to drag us down into the grave every day of our lives. It is by learning to walk in this way that you can overcome these forces. It is equivalent to wearing anti-gravity shoes where you can defy the laws of this world. In the Spirit, you are not subject to the laws to living in a fallen world and can live in genuine peace and harmony with all and everything around you. You can come to know that your higher nature is not subject to the controls that rule the fallen world, no matter what happens in the low places. You can be free experiencing joy and happiness with increasing frequency as you establish your walk and understand the secret to your life.

As I have learned to walk with my heavenly Father, it has enhanced my prayer life as well as everything I do in the natural world. It has far exceeded anything I have learned anywhere on earth. Has it been easy? No, it is a challenge every day to slow down my activities of life on planet Earth and set the time aside to find the quiet place so I can slow my thoughts down to the point of stillness and ascend. Do I accomplish it every day? No! Some days I don't find the time, or if I do just don't seem to be able to clear my head enough to enter fully as I should. However, I do my best to prioritize it every morning without making a religion out of it. What I mean by *religion* is to set a rigid pattern and methodology out of the time I need to spend with God. You can't make a religion out of the "one thing." It defeats the purpose of it. It is about freely spending time in a loving relationship with your Creator.

The first thing you are going to have to come to grips with is accepting Jesus Christ as your Lord and Savior if you want entrance into the gates of heaven. As I said earlier, he is the entrance into the tabernacle which is also a blueprint of how we walk in heaven. It is the first step and access point in order to find the "one thing." If you choose not to accept this point, you will be relegated to experience God through some man-made structure and follow some man, which, for goodness' sake, will lead to nowhere. You just cannot enter nor get past the cherubim with the flaming sword, as Jesus is your ticket into the show. No, you can't hop the fence or sneak in the back door. If you could, the bouncer would smoke you.

Next, you need to be willing to learn to deal with your old nature and learn to deny your flesh from ruling you. The biggest battle for many will be to learn to set the time aside as often as possible to get into a meditative state and learn to retrain your mind. Killing your flesh is nothing more than stopping your external activity and devoting time to walking with God as prescribed in this book.

The fear of dying to self is huge for all of us. We think we are going to have to give up all the pleasures and desires we have to please our flesh. When you spend enough time before you Heavenly Father, you can enjoy all the pleasures and desires that are good for you all the more. The bad stuff will fall away as you will no longer need it to satisfy your lack. It is here that most of the disciples stopped following Jesus when he said "to pick up your cross and follow me." The next fact you will have to accept is to get into the gates of heaven, you must park your fallen nature on the side while your spirit walks on. You will also need to wash yourself in the word of God and learn to not only cleanse your mind but check your spiritual experiences and make sure they line up with the way God created you.

Once you awaken your spirit with the infilling of the Holy Spirit, this will set you free of the law and enable the spiritual gifts to be imparted to you. Your eyes and ears will be opened and you will be able to see where you are walking spiritually and learn to discern what is not of God in the second realm. Remember the second heaven has a mix of both good and evil spirits, and it is by the illumination of God's light that you can see what is operating in the dark and trying to deceive you in order to take you off course. It is only when you get into the third heaven you no longer have to worry about these deceiving spirits. The *only* voice you will hear will be that of God. Once your spirit man is awakened and illuminated, you are ready to be beamed up to ascend the holy mountain into the presence of God.

Once you have come to grips with these things and have worked them out in your mind, you will be dressed in your white robe and ready to walk freely in the atmosphere of heaven. This is the realm of the eagles where both men and women can soar and perceive the things of God clearly, without the filter of self in the way. It is here where the prophets or seers can and have written or spoken to fallen man in order to redeem him from his plight. It is the realm you can mount up and soar on wings of eagles, feeling the breath of God, giving you flight into his heights. It is here you will also learn to write and speak the things of God to others and pour out his unconditional love to the broken and wounded. It is the realm of creativity which comes from the Creator.

Here is how I have learned to do it. This came to me in a vision after I was born again and had already been caught up into heaven. I wanted to know how I can visit heaven again whenever I wanted. God showed me through this vision plus many ensuing visions. I saw a beam of light coming down out of heaven and parting the clouds over my head. It surrounded me and I could feel the incredible warmth of God's love covering me. I then heard his voice telling me to come up here. I then saw myself floating up through the clouds and coming to some gates that were open. I felt unsure, somewhat unworthy, but my heart was pounding to go in. God said to come in, and as I entered I saw a village with people cheering as I walked down the streets. They were celebrating my arrival. I thought, *What is all the fuss for me about?* Following that, I heard God say, "Whenever one of my children finds their way home, my whole kingdom celebrates." It was all quite overwhelming.

The vision went on as I saw myself continuing to walk down the streets of this city and I came to a bridge which I felt I should cross. I looked down and saw a river whose waters were like flowing light. I came to realize this is the river of life. As I got to the other side, I saw the throne of God on a hill, and he beckoned me to come up to him. As I walked up the steps, he picked me up and put me in his lap, and we embraced. My heart was in flames as I felt his passion for me, and I just absorbed as much as I could. The vision ended with God telling me that the beam of light was my key to enter anytime I wanted. Since then, I have found many different pathways and gates into heaven.

If I wanted to visit heaven, usually during my worship experience, I learned that once the Holy Spirit fell on me, I had to shift my thoughts off of myself and still my mind so I could picture the beam of light falling from heaven. It was simply refocusing my thoughts onto the things of God. Once I was able to see the clouds part and the light fall on me, I would then see myself ascending up into heaven and enter the gates. I found I was able to enter at will and learned to apply the seven-step program into a practical worship and meditative experience. One of the keys was to learn to still my mind from all my daily activities and thoughts and turn my focus onto God and the qualities of his kingdom. As I was able to change my focus, my spiritual eyes would open which enabled me to be illuminated and see the things of God. It was then I could see the ancient pathways that led to him—the secret way that is only revealed to your spirit when you are in the Spirit of God.

There are numerous scriptures that speak to shifting your focus and looking up toward heavenly things. Here is a small sample—set your mind on things above and not on things of this world. "Open the eyes of my heart and I lift my eyes up to the mountains where my help comes from." The Bible is so full of things that point to this realm and once you start doing a word and topic study, you will be amazed at where the word of God is pointing. I would recommend if you are not good at navigating your way through the Bible to get a computer Bible program and do word or topic searches. This will enhance your study of the Bible and enable you to see more clearly the living word of God and help your walk in the spirit with him.

If you are able to establish a truly objective view of what God is speaking, you will see some very large signs pointing up the hill and away from the low places. Eventually, it will become so plain you will not know how you missed the large neon sign flashing, saying "This Way Home." The kingdom of God is at hand which is right in front of your face if you learn to see it. Let me say that again! Jesus said, "The kingdom of God is at hand." What he is saying is, "It is here, it is now, and the gates of heaven are open to those who know the secret."

The key is opening the eyes of your heart so your spiritual man can see your way about and follow the highway that leads to heaven. You wouldn't drive on a road blindfolded or walk up a hill in the dark, or you may get hurt. To walk in the spirit, you need to have your eyes wide open and your path illuminated, step 5, by the revelatory word of God. Your heavenly Father is so wanting to show you the way into his kingdom so you can walk with him in the garden he created for you. It will come by the perception of your spiritual mind and the quieting of your carnal mind or intellect. You just need to learn to flip the switch which will become easier and easier the more you walk in this way.

There are many pathways that lead to heaven and many different gates to enter, so what I perceive may be different than what you will see. It is important for you to seek God for your own vision and way to him. I don't want you to take what works for me and try to make it your own. It is only my method which may work for you for a while but hopefully lead you to your own visions of the things of God. Even though I could write volumes about what I have seen in the third heaven, I choose not to tell you because my goal is to lead you to this place so you can have your own experiences. Trust me in this one thing, and that is we so easily turn almost everything into an idol or religion, and it is not my intent to create one for you. I want to set you free from any limitation that may have kept you captive and prevented you from seeing the author of your life.

God is not untouchable! He created us to have relationship with him and also gave us a way to do it. Once you discover the way to him, you will also know what the "one thing" is for your life. The hardest part will be to establish a quiet place in your life so you can experience the quiet place in God. There will be some adjustment with your time, energy, and focus. Without creating some ritualistic experience, you need to set some time aside during your day to seek this place with God. It is not something that has to happen every day. The more often you can do it, the better it will be for you to overcome your problems. If you can make a time to be with God every day and learn to walk with him, it will be even better yet. As I said there is no rule except to learn to spend time with God in this way.

THE "ONE THING"

I have found that as I invest each day and allow more time in this experience and can work through the many distractions, my travel into heaven opens up and deepens. When I first start, my mind is veiled and my eyes are dimly lit. I would say it's like waking up predawn and walking outside where everything is dark. As you sit there and give it enough time, it lightens up until you can see clearly, until it is as bright as the noon sun. There is an adjustment period to transition from the first to third heaven, which takes time. In other words, the more time you can spend, the deeper your experience will be.

You can do it anywhere at anytime once you know the secret. I have learned to be aware of the kingdom of God throughout my day living in the activity of my life. Initially, it is wise to find the quiet place and practice it. I find that good worship music enhances my experience and eases the way into his presence. If you have established a time to pray, meditate, or read your Bible, it will be that much easier to make the transition. It will come once you are able to refocus your thoughts and see yourself walking into the kingdom of heaven. It is a practiced experience that will more easily flow with time. Some days it will seem wide open and easy to enter, while others it will seem difficult. It is okay if you don't get there every time. With quantity comes quality. When you do find your way through the gates, it will be worth all the effort. Some days for me I just can't get my thoughts refocused, so I stop trying and move on with my day.

To apply the "one thing" to your life, it really comes down to devoting the time necessary to understand how the secret works and the passion to see it through. You can't solve the Rubik's Cube if you never pick it up and practice making the secret work so you can get all six sides to line up. The more often you do it, the easier it will become. Eventually, it will seem easy and without effort you are there. Other times, you will be going about your business and sense God's presence or hear him speak to you without even focusing on him. The language of heaven will be more easily understood the more time you spend listening to it. Once you are familiar with it, you will be able to hear it when it speaks even when you are walking in the natural world.

One of the best ways to experience the glory realm of God is to find a ministry or church that embraces this kind of intimate worship. Unfortunately, there are few and far between that will have a heavenly focus. Most of what you will find are churches that focus on keeping people busy supporting their ministry. Most of what they do will have some superficial worship and teaching which puts up the facade of holiness but leaves you empty and confused. I have had some wonderful experiences in conferences and even in some movements, but unfortunately they were short-lived.

If I were to start a meeting or movement, here is what I would consider the prefect worship set. Worship would lead through the three realms using the seven steps. It would start with songs of thanksgiving and praise for our salvation as we enter the gates. It could be songs about Jesus being Lord over our lives and what he did for us. Then songs should progress to the cross and repentance followed with songs that speak to cleansing of your soul being washed clean, also teaching the Bible. Next, worship should lead inside the temple and to the infilling of the Holy Spirit so you can rest in his presence. Once you sense the atmosphere change and God's presence fall and become tangible, sing songs of illumination about opening your eyes, ears, and all your senses opening up; then songs about ascension that speak to going up to God's throne and into the high places. Finally, and where I believe most of the time should be spent, is worship should lead to relationship with God about resting in his arms of love and being face to face with Him. You should be overcome and captured by his presence, and all your senses should be fully alive. It is here you will soak and rest in him.

Worship should be a flow that wakes us up and takes us into the high places to walk with God; worship with the intent of increasing the presence of God until the glory cloud comes. And then walk in it. Don't settle for worship that gives you a marginal experience of God and leaves you wanting for more. If worship doesn't lead you to the throne of God in a breathless state, you are falling short of the mark of what you are called to be. Your worship should have purpose that goes somewhere, not just random songs about Jesus or God that keep you wandering and wondering. Worship shouldn't be about entertaining the people with well-orchestrated sets that have no other purpose. The focus of any type of worship or prayer should lead to the "one thing" and you being able to walk with God in the place you were created to.

HOW I HAVE LEARNED TO
APPLY THE "ONE THING"
TO MY LIFE

Through many years of exploration, I have broken it down to this very simple solution so anyone can do it. My methodology can be adapted to anyone's personal preferences. It is a simple seven-step program!

I am no different than you, just another face in the crowd, someone you would never suspect as being spiritual or even having an ounce of holiness. I am just the average guy working for a living, struggling and trying to make sense of my existence here on earth. I don't walk on water and people don't get healed if they bump into me. I don't sell anointed handkerchiefs or holy water that will heal you or give you a miracle to suddenly make everything better. I have had many failures, been depressed, lost my hope, and had thoughts of suicide. Life has not been a cake walk for me and I have not enjoyed being blessed with lots of money. I work by the sweat of my brow, living in a fallen world, just like you, hoping to find a way to make this life better. I don't pretend to be some great theologian, prophet, or someone of great importance. I much prefer to be a simple guy without a lot of attention or fanfare. It doesn't mean someday I won't get it. For today, I try to be content with what I have, which most importantly is to learn to establish the "one thing" in my life and walk with God more often.

I know every day when I wake up I am as carnal as they come and I will struggle to spend the time I need to get into the Sprit with God. I never said it was easy, that is why I don't sell miracle formulas. It is why what I am talking about is not very popular and no one really wants to talk about it. You have heard it said, "Life is a bitch and then you die." You see, I choose to get the bitch and deal with it before I die and learn to apply the things God created for me so I can make my life a little better each day. As I mature in the things of God, miracles happen, mostly by just being in the atmosphere of holiness. It is not by anything I do, only by what he has allowed me to see and experience. I know for myself this is not only a long journey but a lifelong pursuit to change who I am by discarding the beast within me and walking in my original design. There is a scripture that says narrow is the way that leads to holiness and broad is the path that leads to destruction. It is why many of the disciples left Jesus when he said, "Pick up your cross and follow me." It is why the masses didn't want to go up the mountain and left it to Moses. It is also why in our day, people flock to see a person or event that moves in signs and wonders, or even spend all this time and money to go see a statue shed a tear or drip blood. It's ludicrous to follow a man or place or thing when you can go get it for yourself. But most want to be entertained and will follow the masses instead of taking the narrow way to God. They will seek the work of his hand but not his face.

You have the opportunity to go to the place that will give you all you need or desire and help you mature to the point where miracles can happen around you. It's the unseen realm you should seek, just you and God, so stop chasing man. You can choose how far and deep you want to go with God. You can go all the way like Enoch, who walked with God for three hundred years and he was not, or until his old nature was gone. There is no limit!

I am not saying I will ever arrive at the place Enoch did before I die, but I will continue my relationship with God in this way until either happens. Then I will continue my relationship with God without the pain and suffering that we live with on this side of heaven. I also know I am not the most disciplined person in the world and struggle to practice what I preach, and I don't spend most of my time hidden in some quiet place. I visit heaven as often as I can and try to make my life in this world better. I know when I leave that atmosphere and walk in the natural that the war will be on to steal my joy and peace, yet I also know I have to live in this realm and can't avoid it. It is a daily battle or clash, and my best bet is to get as much of God in me and expand my capacity to keep as much of his qualities with me for as long as possible while I walk around here. Someday I will be free and no longer struggle with the things I do, but until that day, I have to learn to stand up, fight the good fight, and pick up the bed scroll and walk.

I know I have been redeemed through the death of Christ on the cross, and I do my best to understand what that means and apply it to my life. I try not to use an empty word and pretend to be it. I want to learn what it is and how to make it work for me. I know it goes way beyond any concept in my head which I can only grasp with my heart, and at best it is very elusive. I also know that the only way to achieve this is to be in the place where it exists and be before him. It is so easy, yet it is so hard. The way has been made easy for me, but the obstacles in my life stand in my way and make it hard. I want a miracle in a bottle as much as you but have come to realize it doesn't exist. What does exist is a way to the "one thing" in which the secret of your life is; and aside from finding that path, you must also learn to daily walk in it. It is not a drive-through formula where you can get what you want in a few minutes. It is a lifestyle in which you need to learn to walk out.

I know I am lazy and want to take the easy way. Yes, I like to ride the sled to the bottom of the hill and not like to walk back up. I wish I could do nothing and it will all come to me, in which I have tried and found nothing came to me. I know that applying this "one thing" to my life takes a lot of effort and time, but its rewards are worth it. It is life or death for me now through which I choose I will reap daily.

When I walk down the street or around the lake by my home, I look into peoples' eyes and attempt to say hi, but what I see is people filled with problems. I see many who are hiding behind something and avoid my glances—those who are insecure, fearful, depressed, worried, angry, isolated and lonely, or with some other hang-up. I see very few that are happy and are open to say hi back. I see many who are looking for an answer to their lives and problems and don't have a clue where to turn. I am saddened that I do have a solution for them and have no way of telling them. I know it is the "one thing," where all these issues can be resolved as they walk in this way. When I am there, all of the same issues that I have seem to melt away. The negative voices stop speaking, my thoughts are free, and my feelings are at peace. All I find are all the good qualities of life, which I can enjoy while in his presence. As I said, it is when I return from my visit that I have to deal with living in this world. Yet, the more I visit, the better I am able to deal with all of it. The less I visit, the stronger the voices of condemnation, the negative thoughts, and ill feelings get.

I also believe that we are not called to live our days out in the quiet places on some mountainside avoiding all the problems in the realm of man. We are called to bring forth what we get from God and pour it out to hopefully have some impact to the broken around us. The first part of our journey is to find our way up the mountain and find the place we can walk with God and establish our relationship. If we choose to stay there, we will never complete the second part of our journey, which is to go back down the mountain to the valley and touch mankind despite all the persecutions and betrayals we will have to deal with.

In a sense, I wish I didn't have to come back to the realm of man and be assaulted by his ways. I am not a monastery type of person and don't believe in living isolated on a mountaintop somewhere behind closed doors. I believe in what is still good in mankind and want to be a part of the solution, despite the assaults that happenonce in a while. If I didn't want to live in this realm, then I could never accomplish the other thing. What is the other thing? Well, that will be the sequel to this book called "The Other Thing."

The way I practice and apply it to my life is to take the key that opens up heaven to enhance my experience of God whenever I pray or meditate, worship, read the Bible, or any other time I want to enter. The *key* is the light which I see falling from heaven. God is light, his love is light, which are some of his many qualities. It is in the light where our spiritual eyes and ears are illuminated to perceive God's nature and where we are able to walk to and with him. I have repeated this point a few times, and it is worth emphasizing for you to grasp the importance of you opening up your imagination and seeing in the Spirit. It is okay to visualize, imagine, picture, and practice anything else that enhances your spiritual experience with God as long as you have your foundation in place. The candlestick, the fifth step, represents light and illumination. Jesus says he is the light to shine in a dark world to lead you. The

Bible is full of scriptures that talk about light as one of God's qualities.

Your foundation is knowing the word of God well enough to check what you are hearing or seeing in the spiritual realm as well as through other people. When we get caught up in the second heaven, you must remember that it is the realm of the mix, where both good and dark spiritual forces exist and where deception is possible. I have seen some people get really goofy trying to get in the spirit by not having their foundation in the Word. This realm is where the psychics and spiritualists operate, but without any foundation in the word of God, they are walking with demonic and fallen spirits. They call them "angels of light" which appear to be from God and speak to your fallen mind, just like the serpent spoke to Adam and Eve. There is a lot of work in taking the time to read your Bible and mediate on its meaning, but this will lay the foundation to build your house in the heights with God. I don't tell you this to give you fear but to help you plan your journey well. Remember, this is the part of the third step and training ground school to prepare you to know how to fly.

I start off my pray or worship time with thanking the Lord for all he did and then inviting the Holy Spirit to come and wash over me to cleanse me from the dirt I pick up living in the world or the stuff hidden inside of me. I find playing intimate worship music definitely enhances my experience as I can quiet myself down and listen to the words. I always try to still my mind of all the things I need to do at that moment and refocus it on the things of God. Once I am able to quiet down, I start to picture the beam of light falling on me and then I begin to see myself walking up a path or soaring upwards. I have seen many pathways up into heaven. Sometimes I see the same way, while on others I see different ones. I try to control it as little as possible, just long enough to get there, and then I let it go for God to take over. My goal is to get through the first and second heavens and into the third where I can walk with him. Once I am able, I just rest in him and enjoy our time together; the place where we walk and talk, and he shows me things. He loves to bring me into his map room to show me things about my life and the world I live in. It is the place of revelation and prophecy. It is the place of creativity.

While I have been writing this book, I have been seeing myself taking off like an eagle and soaring into the heights with my wings stretched open on the breath of God. Every time I get up in this realm, I see scrolls handed to me which I take by the talons, and as I am soaring, I shred pieces off and eat and digest them. I have found that when God speaks to me and I get a thought for this book and am not in a position to write it down, it doesn't fade away, but I retain it until I can write it down. Normally, in the past, when I received revelation, if I didn't write it down right away, I would later say, "That was a good thought, but what was it?" I have found in my meditations with God that he is feeding my spirit, and I am able to retain it. I have also found the more I can focus on God and not get distracted by my life, the more intense my experience with him is, where his words burn into my mind and are not so easily forgotten.

Some days it is easy to connect with God; it seems in a moment I am there walking with him and all my senses are alive, while other times it is very difficult to break through as my senses are dull and my focus is everywhere else. Sometimes my thoughts are on what I need to get done today or on my worries, and I can't seem to shift them. It becomes a wrestling match and it is then I need to use the key and get my thoughts lifted up and see the beam of light parting the clouds and feeling the Spirit fall on me. Once I am able to battle through, it opens up. If I can't, I just move on with my day and not worry about it. If it is not happening, I walk away and deal with what I have to. I find there are a lot of things that can get in the way of walking with God, and one way or another they have to be dealt with—either I break through or I go deal with them until I can get them behind me so next time they don't carry weight and keep me grounded.

This whole model is something that you will develop over time becoming sensitive to the things of God. You never know when a heavenly moment will happen in your life, when the windows of heaven will open and the presence of God will pour in. It is so easily missed if your spirit is not sensitized to the things of the Spirit and the atmosphere of heaven. When you have spent enough time walking in the realm where God dwells, it becomes that much easier to perceive when the supernatural invades the natural. When you are able to walk through the gates freely walking in the third heaven, becoming more sensitive to your created nature and your connection to God, you will be able to recognize more easily when God opens the windows and pours out on us.

There is a difference between the windows and gates of heaven. The windows are openings where God pours out to us in a fallen world and brings light to the darkness of our internal house. God will only use the windows to pour out his light occasionally, because he doesn't want us to get comfortable where we are separated from him in the first heaven. He uses these moments of outpouring to remind us of whom we are and where we really belong. They are sort of wakeup calls for us to rise up or mount up on hind's feet and leap and bound into the heights and enter the gates to walk with him in the third heaven. The gates are designed for us to walk through and enter his kingdom. The windows are where God comes to us and enters the kingdom of man, and the gates are where we go to God and enter the kingdom of heaven.

The "one thing" is not only your first commandment relationship with God but also learning to walk through the gates of heaven to walk in the original creation and rest in God's realm where you can love him with your whole being. Once you understand this method of approaching God, the secrets of your life will be opened up where you will be able to unfold a lot of the hidden mysteries. You will also be able to problem solve and clear up many of the issues in your life that lead to pain and suffering. As I said earlier, this is not a one-shot deal but a new lifestyle in which you will have to learn to shift your focus from the cares of this world onto the things of God's world. He did not design us to live under the clouds in a fallen world. He did design us to live above the clouds in the brilliance of his light where everything is transparent and clear.

I am going to say a few things that will get the religious folks or Pharisees up in arms and on their high horse. The reason I keep harping on this point is that through my whole Christian experience, I have encountered your ridicule, accusations, and persecutions whenever I talk about anything out of the box of your understanding, when it doesn't fit into your little tiny grid of the structures you set up about God. You are no different than the people who had no clue to who Jesus was even though it was clearly written in the scriptures. God came in a different way than what they thought, thus assaulting their intellect; so they justified and attacked Jesus as some heretic, wanting to get rid of him because he so threatened their whole belief system and corrupted hearts.

One of the best things I have ever done is the practice of yoga stretching which I learned in college before I became a Christian. I have learned to apply the exercise, quieting down of my mind and impulses and meditations to enhance my experience with God. I always take an open approach to anything I do and believe God will show me what is of him and what is not. I had to learn to separate most of the Hindu philosophy from the beneficial components of practicing yoga. I have received much criticism and scrutiny from many people in the Christian circles over the years as their fear of deception outweighed their ability to see if there was any benefit in what I was saying that could help them with their experience in getting closer to God.

The key elements to awakening your spirit so it can be sensitive and perceive the realms and things of God are some form of physical exercise to awaken you and make your mind alert, then transitioning by quieting your mind down and changing your focus from the world to the kingdom of God and then opening up your eyes and ears to hear what God is saying to you. Exercise, meditation, and visualization are all valuable in becoming still and walking in the Spirit with God. Visualization is nothing more than learning to exercise the senses of your spirit. If your focus is on God, then it is a wonderful enhancement to your spiritual journey with him.

I tell you the truth that unless you can overcome your fears, you can't enter the place of rest. You will be an endless wonderer, just like the Israelites who feared the giants they had to face to enter the promised land. What are your giants? You will have to discover and face them in order to enter and find the "one thing." Some of the biggest giants you will have to face are your ego and religious structures. Your arrogance in thinking you know better and have the answers will keep you from the goal. Many of the other giants will be your insecurities, worries, and fears in the emotional realm. Of course we can't forget the lusts of our flesh and materialism. All these pursuits can keep you so preoccupied that you will never find the time or a place to do what it takes to enter the gates of heaven and walk with God.

Your heart is like a lump of cold Play-Doh that needs to be massaged daily to become soft and pliable. The softer and more pliable your heart becomes, the easier it is for God to mold you into what he originally created you for. By great effort, your heart will soften, but once you stop it will become cold and hard again. Another dynamic of the "one thing" is that you need to practice and exercise your spiritual muscles often in order to continue your journey in the place where you can continue to grow and prosper not only in the spiritual but also in the natural.

COMPLETING THE CYCLE

If you are able to break the old patterns and complete the cycle, you will find the place of rest you have always desired. Once you are able to complete the cycle, you will be able to live life as you were originally created to.

Earlier, I said Jesus was the wisest man to ever walk the face of the earth. Some believe it was Solomon, who was blessed with great wisdom from God. However, he squandered it on the desires of his flesh and the cares of the world. Jesus walked with God and was one with him until the point where he was able to lay down his flesh for all our sakes. His great wisdom was in overcoming the fallen nature with all its temptations until he reached the point where he broke the cycle and could operate in the Spirit simultaneously while walking in the world. He was so able to operate in the nature of God while walking on earth that wherever he went, he impacted those he came into contact with both in a positive and negative way. The presence of God was so strong it either drove you to God, where you experienced healing and blessings, or away from

THE ONE THING AND SECRET OF LIFE

him, where you became bitter and resentful. Wisdom is from God; and the more closely we can become like him, the more wisdom we attain and learn to exercise in the here and now.

The number 7 represents perfection and the completion of the cycle, but it also represents rest. You must learn to rest in him and walk in your created nature while you put all your animal instincts and beastly pursuits aside during your pray time. This is called *repentance*, step 2 in the tabernacle experience. Your flesh seeks material satisfaction while your spirit seeks heavenly fulfillment, where you need to find a balance so you can satisfy both. To break the cycle of man, you must take the seventh step and rest in it so you can absorb God's nature to make your life more satisfying each and every day. Your life will be increasingly blessed and prosperous once you learn to break the cycle and walk in the way you were created to walk.

The number 6 is the number of man. It also represents the cycle of man working and slaving by the work of his own hands for his own gain and satisfaction. Man's fallen nature is the beast nature. The beast nature and mark of the beast is 666, which is the perpetual cycle of man. In other words, man works by the sweat of his brow and continues in his own ways and never finds the place of rest. It is man ceaselessly operating in his own works—the work of his mind and his hand—and trusting in himself, never breaking the cycle to take the seventh step to rest and walk with God. Oh, *wow*, that's a revelation!

Self = sin.

Union with God = sinless.

Choose life (God) and you will live. Choose death (self) and you will die.

Hopefully this will simplify the need to seek God first in your life.

You are the battleground and the war wages on within you. Your flesh hates the things of the Spirit and will do all it can to resist you entering the place of rest where you can feed your spirit. That is how stupid and dense the beast nature is within each of us, to push away what it really needs to be satisfied while it seeks its own pleasures that lead to its destruction.

Do you have cherubim with flaming swords blocking your entrance into the place your heart craves? You must learn to break the cycle of yourself and walk in the Spirit. The key is Christ! If you can't accept the way Jesus laid out for you, then you can only worship God from the outside at best. The second key is the Holy Spirit being filled and covered which gives you your new garment, the white robe of righteousness, that allow you to enter. If you have the keys, you will need to learn how to use them so you can open the gates and walk into the high places with God and begin to allow your spirit to grow and be the dominant factor in your life. The keys are like a VIP pass—when presented will allow you to pass by the angel as he lifts his sword out of your way and grant you entrance into the most amazing place you will ever experience.

You have to grasp these two truths to enter the atmosphere where you can rest from all the stresses and pressures we face each and every day. The first is entering the gate, which is Christ, who was God incarnate in the flesh. "I tell you the truth I am the gate for the sheep.... I am the gate whoever enters through me will be saved. He will come in and go out and find pasture," John 10:7 and 9 (NIV). The sheep are God's people, who choose to seek, find, and follow God and his ways. The pasture is the kingdom of God where you have free access to that realm, only through Jesus. "I am the way and the truth and the life. No one comes to the Father except through me," John 14:6 (NIV).

The second part is the Holy Spirit, where God has come in the Spirit to touch fallen man and cover and protect us as we move through the second heaven. The Holy Spirit is our vehicle to ascend into the third heaven. Jesus gets you in, while the Holy Spirit gets you up. Once you learn to walk in the Spirit, you can walk freely through the gates of heaven and walk with your heavenly Father, author and creator of life. In God's master plan, Jesus was going home to be with him while he sent the Holy Spirit for all times to come to those who called out to him and asked to be filled. It is God's purpose to use the Holy Spirit to guide us back to him (John 14:15–31). These are just a small sampling of what the Bible says in regard to finding your way home to discover the "one thing."

In his book *My Utmost for His Highest*, Oswald Chambers writes for October 10th, "The path to spiritual growth is by atmosphere and not by intellectual reasoning." In order to enter the gates of heaven, you must lay down your own intellect, carnal thinking, and put on your spiritual mind so you can enter the atmosphere where you can absorb the qualities and put on the nature God designed for you by nothing more than you just being there. Imagine that you don't have to work for it or do anything but just show up, be there, and rest in it. When you can find your way into this realm, your heart will burst into flames, experiencing a love that is beyond anything you have ever experienced anywhere in this world. Your perspective of things also increases the higher up the mountain you learn to walk.

People of the Word get so caught up in reading the Bible that they never got off the pages and learn to walk out its intent. You can't fly if you are a perpetual ground school student. The Bible is a mere instruction book on how to fly and walk with God in the spirit into the heights with him and experience the unconditional love he created for you to feed on, like Jonathan Livingston Seagull, who got up and flew where no one said he should, leaving those on the ground who condemned him. In order to return to the place of your creation, you must learn to walk in the spiritual heights and stop listening to the voices on the ground who wants to keep you bound by their beliefs.

"The bird who flies highest sees farthest." I don't know who said this, but as you learn to soar into the heights with God, you will experience views and perspectives you never imagined possible. Also I heard it said, "The bird who flies highest falls hardest." One of these sayings is fear-based while the other is adventure-based. Which would you rather do, explore the heights of possibilities or sit on the ground while you worry about what could go wrong? I have chosen to be an adventurer, one who wants to explore the depths of God and discover the mysteries others have feared venturing toward. Why allow fear to keep you from all God has for you? This is why it is so important to put your trust in your Creator and allow him to be in control of your experiences. Don't allow the words of others, the council flock, to dictate who you are and where you will go in the Spirit. Worrying about your image, what you will look like before others, or what they will say is a death sentence. There is nothing keeping you from entering the gates of heaven this very moment but yourself. You are free; you just need to let go of all that holds you down and ascend the holy mountain of God.

God rejoices when one of his children find their way home. The whole kingdom of God celebrates when you walk through the gates of heaven finding your way into your heavenly home. He loves to show you things and will give you revelations that cannot only change your life but also the world you live in. In this place, you are not insignificant—you are great, wanted, and needed. You have a great mission before you, and only in this atmosphere of revelation can you find it. Once you have completed the cycle and take the seventh step, a whole new world will open up and leave you in awe. It is a place where you will find all the missing pieces of the puzzle of your life. The more often you visit, the more missing pieces you will find and perhaps one day you will complete the giant jigsaw puzzle of your life. You will find a level of unconditional love that you never thought possible. It will leave you breathless.

In the natural world where we spend most, if not all, of our time, and where all we ever find are droplets of conditional love, our hearts are love sponges looking to soak up any droplet of love that they can. It is no wonder our spirits are atrophied like some plant that is thrown in some dark corner of the house where it is devoid of direct sunlight. Even though it receives water and nutrients, it still gets brown and shriveled up because it lacks light. Our spirit doesn't get its nutriments from earthly things; it is designed to be in God's light, which is his unconditional love—a light from God that feeds, strengthens, and builds up our higher nature which leads to happiness, peace, security and all the things we dream about while living in this fallen world. It is the only way to overcome sin. Sin is not the issue, the lack of God's direct light is. As his light shines in our soul, transformation takes place by nothing more than being in the atmosphere of love.

Breaking the cycle is not done by trying to lead a sinless life, which can't be done. It can only come by completing the cycle, taking the seventh step, finding your way home to live in the original creation, and just resting in the presence of pure love. There is nothing else you have to do, only find your way there and learn to rest in it. Once you are able to find the "one thing" and walk in that way, you will see how simple it all is.

Just one more thought: I want to talk about the three perishes in the Old Testament. There are three reasons why people perish, according to the word of

God. Those who are aware of how we perish focus on the last in order, which is, "My people perish for a lack of knowledge." The other two are, "My people perish for a lack of a plan and a lack of vision." Let's start with the first and most important of these.

"My people perish for a lack of a plan."

The "one thing" is the plan! The plan was written in the tabernacle and the seven steps on how to approach and walk with God. Once you can grasp the plan God has laid out for you, you will fulfill the other two. God's plan is not complicated; just requires you to be willing to humble yourself and lay down your arrogant pride to be able to take the seven steps. You will perish if you are unwilling. You fail because you are in the way of following his plan. Your Heavenly Father has made the plan very simple and clear, and all you need to do is follow it to receive vision and knowledge.

"My people perish for lack of a vision."

It is at the fifth step in the plan and place of illumination that your eyes are open and you receive vision. It is no wonder the majority of the world is perishing and dying in pain and suffering. It is because they are blind, having their spiritual eyes scaled over by living and eating of the wrong tree. The density of your flesh, like a foreskin that needs circumcision, has your spiritual senses dulled or dark. If you were blind and deaf in the

natural, would you try to go about the city without a
guide? Well, you do in life if you have not received your
vision from above.

"MY PEOPLE PERISH FOR
A LACK OF KNOWLEDGE."

Once you receive your vision, you can see and hear
your way about the kingdom of God and attain the
knowledge you need to deal with the issues of your
life. Knowledge can help you overcome anything you
face and have to deal with. Knowledge in this case is
wisdom from heaven. Knowledge increases as your
spirit increases and your flesh decreases. You see, the
more you seek the kingdom of God, the more aware
and perceptive you will become in understanding the
secrets of life.

Completing the cycle requires you to follow the plan
and get your eyes and ears to open so you can come to
the place where your understanding of life will unfold,
and you can overcome all and any problems that plague
you in this life. I tell you the truth, once you are able to
complete the cycle, you will be in utter awe of what you
will sense and feel and how the quality of your life will
improve on this side of heaven. You will be on your way
to be an overcomer—one who conquers this life.

CONCLUSION

The main thing I have to deal with is myself, every day, every moment of my life. There is no choice in the matter! I can avoid it, live in denial, or pretend everything is good. However, when I awake in the morning, I have to deal with my life and the fruit of my decisions. Not only do I have to deal with myself but those around me have to deal with my choices, whether good or bad. I impact not only me but those that live in the world I touch. The greater my sphere of influence, the more important it will be for me to take a hard look in the mirror and see what needs to be fixed.

What I eat or drink and what I say and think will determine the outcome of my life. I have to live by the choices I make, and they will lead me to prosperity or failure, blessings or curses. If I choose wisely, I can have a life of abundance and peace. If I choose wrongly, then I set the tone for aimlessly wandering in the wilderness of pain and suffering and experience death before it's time. I can't blame my parents, circumstances, and the conditions we live in for my lack, because through all of the problems I face daily, I have the ability to choose wisely. This will lead us to overcome, conquer, and be victors over the hand we were dealt. God gave you the right of choice, which by it you can choose life or death and heaven or hell, and thus you will experience. The most hopeless of situations can be overcome by the right choices and the will to persevere until you arrive at the other side and find the joy and happiness you were designed to have. There are many choices and many ways, and it is easy to get confused and lost. Choose the "one thing" that can lead you to the promised land.

Have you heard of the expression, "You are your own worst enemy?" Me, myself, and I are in the way of finding the riches and blessings this life has to offer in the here and now. The key to dealing with yourself is to learn to get out of yourself. The best way to get out of yourself is to focus on the only thing that can bring transformation to your broken image, and that is the "one thing"—walking with and loving God. To make positive change in who I have become, I need to stop looking inward at what's wrong with me and focus outward on the author and creator of my life and the design for how I should live. The more time I spend walking with God in the loving relationship he allows me to have with him, the more my old broken image is replaced with the new one and my image is restored. As I continue in seeking the "one thing" and following in his ways, I can be completely healed and made new.

If it is not God that I seek, the creator of my DNA, then who or what? Do I seek many ways and many answers and live in confusion, or do I want to simplify and seek the one and only thing that can bring real change in my life? If I have a poor self-image and I don't recognize that "one thing" that can give me what I need and feed my soul, I will gravitate toward other things that will only give me temporary satisfaction. If I choose to be like some other person that may be my hero or has an image I aspire to be like, what do I do when they fail me or fall? If it is something that I try to quench my appetite with, like money, style, position, or some worldly form of security, then what do I do when they falter? These are all temporary satisfactions and leave my soul and spirit malnourished. It is no wonder people with so much have train wrecks for lives, because they are seeking the wrong thing. You see, if I take on someone else's image, I will dress like them, walk like them, talk like them, and pretend to be them. If it is some style, trend or thing, then my image has a shelf life of how long it is "in." I am totally lost and will find massive disappointments as all the other things I seek to satisfy my needs fails. If I let the opinions of others mold me because of my insecurities and the need of acceptance, I am seeking the wrong thing, which is the approval of men. I am nothing more than a mere shadow of who I truly am. There is only one thing that matters, and it is a God who loves you as you are, unconditionally!

Each of us has to overcome the self-absorption that leads us to believe we don't need any help from anyone or anything, and the self-centered, arrogant attitude that makes us feel we are better than others. We can't even see how much of a turnoff this is to others and one of the most dangerous places to be. When your self-made utopia falls apart, whom do you turn to? When your world falls apart, where do you go? When you fail yourself, what do you do? You retreat in yourself believing you can't trust anyone or anything, when in reality you should be looking at yourself as the culprit.

You've heard it said, "The Truth will set you free!" But what is the truth, and where do you find it? Is there one central truth for you? I tell you today there is a truth designed for you that will lead to freedom and lasting happiness, and it is found in the "one thing."

You see, there is only one truth for you, and unless you can find that "one thing" that can give you that revelation, you will perpetuate in your journey looking for answers in a lost world. Only in your relationship with God can you find the truth which will restore your image. Your created nature will rise up and overcome the fallen nature the world placed on you. The answers come when you spend time with him, rest in him and be his friend. This was the original design by God in the garden before it was lost in the fall. We have been given the right to return to this place, yes, on this side of heaven, through Jesus. Jesus opened the veil through the cross that separated us from God via Adam's disobedience. Now you can walk with God in the cool breeze of the day and talk with him. As we walk with perfection, we absorb that nature and thus become perfect—a perfection that is much higher than our puny little minds can grasp from our perspective on earth.

Once you find the "one thing" and pursue it, whole-heartedly, your life will never be the same and will change for the better. As you continue your journey through the wilderness and overcome obstacles and face trials with him by your side, you will be made strong. You will learn to stand tall in the face of anything that comes your way and be an overcomer. You will be known as you are fully known.

There is only "one thing," one very simple thing who has the answer for you, and that is your Creator and designer of your very own and personal DNA. I hope you can find the place I have talked about in this book and learn to walk and talk it out. Then and only then will you know what I am talking about; the rest is illusion! If you do, not only will your life be transformed for the better, but you will have the ability to reach out to those around you and help a dying world. The world will be a better place just because of you.

As your spirit is sensitized to the things of God, you will get dreams, visions, and hear from God. You can walk and talk with your Heavenly Father who always has the time for you as long as you have the time for him. Keep asking him the questions that are on your mind or heart, and he will answer. The minute you stop is when you start to allow gravity to pull you back down toward the grave. Don't build an altar at any step along the way and create God in your image, as many have, and don't let them clip your wings. The voices in the lower realms want to keep you grounded and away from the "one thing" that will show you the truth, which will unfold the secrets of your life. You were meant to fly, so mount up on wings of eagles, soar into the heights were other eagles fly, into the realm of eagles.

Once your image is made whole through your journey to the "one thing" and the transformation process that happens by just being in that atmosphere, then you can start working on the "other thing." The "other thing" will start a whole new cycle where you can take everything you have learned before God and have it tested and tried. This will start the process of seasoning, which is the testing of what you have learned in the high places while trying to live with them in the low places.

The whole of creation is open before you and there is nothing that can hold you back but yourself. It is now up to you to pursue the "one thing" that can restore you so you can live your life as you were designed to. Once you experience the breath of God on your face, which will leave you breathless and in awe, you will have started the process of complete restoration. You will never be the same.

AFTERTHOUGHT

There are many prophecies and references to how the end will come. Many have tried to figure it out. There are numerous TV shows depicting their version of doomsday. Yes, everyone is jumping on the bandwagon of end-time scenarios. Must be big money in it!

The Bible, however, makes many references to all people awakening and coming to a full knowledge of God and the old order of things passing away so we can live in the new order. I hope to keep our focus here, for us to gain a full knowledge of God and then the rest won't matter. I hope this book aids and serves as a prelude to man's awakening to the way God created us, and for us to walk with him and love him.

One final thought: the kingdom of God is a lot closer than you many realize. It is at hand!

Please visit Bob Cerami on his website, www.exploringheaven.com. You are welcome to comment or leave thoughts about this book. You can also inquire about speaking engagements.

.

CPSIA information can be obtained
at www.ICGtesting.com
Printed in the USA
BVOW11s1603120318
510355BV00029B/1118/P